The

JOURNEY

of

CONVERSION

The
JOURNEY
of
CONVERSION

GARY J. COLEMAN

DESERET
BOOK
SALT LAKE CITY, UTAH

Library of Congress Cataloging-in-Publication Data

Coleman, Gary (Gary J.)

    The journey of conversion : a renewed invitation to come unto Christ / Gary J. Coleman.

      p.   cm.

    Includes bibliographical references and index.

    ISBN 1-59038-161-0 (pbk.)

    1. Coleman, Gary (Gary J.)   2. Church of Jesus Christ of Latter-day Saints—Biography.   3. Mormon Church—Biography.   I. Title.

BX8695.C55A3 2003

289.3'092—dc21   2003008924

Printed in the United States of America   8006-7116
Banta, Menasha, WI

10 9 8 7 6 5 4 3 2 1

To my wife, Judy, my best friend.

The field is white already to harvest; and lo,

he that thrusteth in his sickle with his might,

the same layeth up in store that he perisheth not,

but bringeth salvation to his soul.

DOCTRINE AND COVENANTS 4:4

CONTENTS

PREFACE

This is not an official publication of The Church of Jesus Christ of Latter-day Saints, nor was it written at the request of the Church officials. Thus it does not represent official doctrine or statements on these matters. The author alone is responsible for its contents.

Preparing this manuscript for publication required literally hundreds of changes, revisions, additions, deletions, and most of all advice from others over a long period of time. My dear companion, Judy, was a wonderful helpmeet and counselor through the entire effort to bring the work to this point. Our daughter Kolette Coleman Hall gave inspired and extraordinary assistance in all phases of preparing the manuscript. Kent England Coleman labored with me for hours to address format and content. Kara Coleman Liston, Kyle England Coleman, Kory England Coleman, and Kamron Scott England Coleman all eagerly encouraged the outcome of this labor for many months, and I thank our family for their important contributions.

I am truly grateful for talented sisters who kindly provided help at one point or another on the many renditions. I express my thanks to Patty Reid and Daisy Troyo for their support, suggestions, and application of writing skills during months and even years of attention to this ongoing process. I also thank those who contributed experiences and personal accounts of missionary efforts for giving permission to use their material.

Sheri Dew initially received this manuscript and was willing to commit the resources of Deseret Book Company to this project. Cory Maxwell gave me expert backing on how to proceed with the publication. Jack M. Lyon has projected his enthusiasm and approval since the very beginning of the editing process. I sincerely thank those who read the manuscript and recommended it to Deseret Book's board of directors as well as those who made significant contributions to help this project come to fruition.

INTRODUCTION

At age twenty-one, while I was a practicing Catholic and a student at Washington State University, I began the important process of conversion to The Church of Jesus Christ of Latter-day Saints. Despite the traditions I had been taught, it was the power and conviction in the words and actions of members of the Church and the truths they shared with me that drew me to the restored gospel. They were living their lives in harmony with the teachings of the Bible and the Book of Mormon and other literature they provided me. Since that day in 1962, I have searched for ways to influence others to participate in the restored gospel of Jesus Christ. Not having served a full-time mission as a young man, but having a deep desire to share the gospel, I know that as members of the Church we can accomplish this wonderful service to others. My personal experience is strengthened by hundreds of missionary experiences as well. The feelings of joy that come from helping others find the true teachings of Christ are a manifestation of the power of the gospel. My experiences as a full-time mission president have only strengthened my resolve to be a better participant in this important part of the gospel. I believe that there are keys that will help us unlock doors to find joy in this effort, and these key points will be discussed throughout this book. Others who are missionary minded have fostered additional principles. Every idea, effort, and suggestion used will help hasten this vital, latter-day work.

Our efforts to assist in the conversion of others is the Lord's work. The Lord has commanded the members of His church to raise the warning voice to all peoples of the earth. President Gordon B. Hinckley has counseled, "If we will go forward, never losing sight of our goal, speaking ill of no one, living the great principles we know to be true, this cause will roll in majesty and power to fill the earth. Doors now closed to the preaching of the gospel will be opened. The Almighty, if necessary, may have to shake nations to humble them and cause them to listen to the servants of the living God. Whatever is needed will come to pass" ("Look to the Future," *Ensign,* November 1997, 67).

President Hinckley has further said, "The process of bringing new people into the Church is not the responsibility alone of the missionaries. They succeed best when members become the source from which new investigators are found. . . . Let there be cultivated an awareness in every member's heart of his own potential for bringing others to a knowledge of the truth. Let him work at it. Let him pray with great earnestness about it" ("Find the Lambs, Feed the Sheep," *Ensign,* May 1999, 104). This effort may well be one of the trials of our faith.

This book is for you, the member of The Church of Jesus Christ of Latter-day Saints and your long-time member friends who have the joy and blessing of sharing the gospel of Jesus Christ. It is also for your prospective-member friend who is seeking what you have in the restored gospel. Through sharing this gospel you will come to know what the Savior meant when He said, "How great shall be your joy with him in the kingdom of my Father" (D&C 18:15). I have attempted to weave the doctrinal and social conversion process together as I have experienced them over the past forty years of being a convert to The Church of Jesus Christ of Latter-day Saints. In each of the chapters I will cite a few verses from a sacred scriptural record, the Book of Mormon, which I believe will help lay this foundation for true conversion to Jesus Christ. These scriptural witnesses about our Savior in the Book of Mormon, Another Testament of Jesus Christ, are placed in the book to inspire you to reflect upon the doctrines of Christ. I challenge you to put your trust in the Lord and share what you have been given.

Converts accept at least two major life-changing experiences upon entering The Church of Jesus Christ of Latter-day Saints. The first is doctrinal conversion. The missionary discussions and your conversations introduce an interested person to all kinds of new religious concepts, heaven-revealed truths, and, most of all, the doctrine of Christ. The Spirit will testify to the honest in heart, during the conversations, that the doctrines are true. Promptings of the Spirit are readily available to the honest in heart to help them recognize the true doctrines of Christ. As each lesson is concluded, the invitation is again extended to the participants to ponder and pray about these truths. This is part of the process of doctrinal conversion, and it will continue for the rest of our mortal lives.

Another life-changing experience that occurs for a convert is the social conversion that will take place. We teach converts that most of what they have known and enjoyed in their religious background and training, up to this time, will not be thrown away but added upon and enlightened. President Hinckley has said this about the beliefs of others: "I hope we can be good neighbors to those not of our faith. I hope we can recognize the good that other churches do and add to that good as we have opportunity to do so" (*Atlanta Journal Constitution*, 23 June 2000). This social conversion is also a process that will likely affect every fiber of a person's being. Think of it! Parents, brothers, sisters, children, and extended family are affected by religious change. Friends, associates, fellow workers, religious leaders, social groups, and classmates may be aware of the change. Converts' worship experience, free time, and all things about them will be affected. What they eat and drink, what they wear, where they go, who they meet, how they speak, and what entertainment they seek will undergo a transition influenced by the Spirit of the Lord upon their lives. Because these changes are so pronounced in every part of our social fabric, a convert's beliefs must be founded on the true doctrine of Christ. A convert must be firmly anchored on the rock of the Savior and His church so that the storms, hail, and winds of life that often come with conversion will not prevail. However, these changes are often challenging and must be understood by members of the Church in order to provide the necessary support that converts desperately need after baptism. We must remember that our missionary effort does not stop at baptism; it only begins.

I have become a witness of the living Christ in these latter days through the doctrine and social conversion process that has occurred along the path that leads to eternal life. I was once a prospective member and in my younger years had no idea I would go through this powerful conversion process. A person not yet a member but preparing to be a member is a prospective member. As you will come to find out, my spiritual education began as a child, continued throughout my growth as a prospective member, progressed further when I was baptized, and has never ceased.

It is the profound spiritual power derived from reading and pondering and praying about the message of the Book of Mormon that leads us to take courage in our hearts and share the restored gospel. Our friends, associates, and even family members have been "kept from the truth because they know not where to find it" (D&C 123:12). They will be brought to the knowledge of the truths of the restored gospel by the power of the Holy Ghost as promised by the prophet Moroni in the Book of

Mormon (Moroni 10:4–5). In this book you will find principles that you can apply to the missionary experiences you have with those in your circle of influence. Believe it is possible, for if you do, you can play a necessary role in establishing the true church in the lives of your friends and associates. You can strengthen your brothers and sisters in their conversion to the Lord. Follow me down my road to conversion and find ways to bring forth the restored gospel with others. Mine has been a journey of many decades, sustained progress, some heartache, but much joy. I invite you to join me on this life-changing journey.

1

BEGINNING WITH THE TRADITIONS OF OUR FATHERS

My parents were devout Christian people who were members of the Catholic Church. I was born in Wenatchee, Washington, and lived my youth in Brewster and Bridgeport, small farming communities bordering the Columbia River north of Wenatchee. Forty-four days after my birth I was baptized in the usual manner under the care of the local parish priest. My baptism was witnessed by my parents along with an uncle who was invited to be my godfather and my grandmother who was an ever-watchful godmother. My middle name, Jerome, was from Saint Jerome, a patron saint in the Catholic tradition of monks and scholars. To my knowledge, this religion was a strongly established tradition in my paternal ancestry for many generations.

For the next twenty-one years I was reared and instructed under the influence of my family's adherence to these religious teachings. My parents raised their five children, I being the eldest, in what they understood to be righteous paths. I am indebted to them for the training and care I received under their guidance. If it had not been as sound as it was, perhaps I would never have cared about seeking the true gospel of Jesus Christ.

Innocent as we all are in the beginning of our mortal journey, we are nevertheless subject to the traditions of our fathers in all things, and surely in our religious upbringing. At age six I received a gift from Grandmother Coleman, who had a hand in my spiritual growth as she stayed with us on the farm for extended periods of time. She was a devout Catholic, and her interest in my development was heightened as I showed promise of becoming a priest myself. My mother recorded the event in my history as follows: "Received first rosary beads from Grandmother Coleman and said the rosary by himself the first night he received it." This was the beginning of a tradition of reciting rote prayers from memory. I would continue this practice tens of thousands of times in my worship experience. For many years we drove to Brewster to attend church events. During the Chief Joseph Dam construction, we had services in the Bridgeport theater, and this was followed by the building of a new Catholic church in Bridgeport, Washington, in the mid-1950s. It was across the street from the home where I lived during my late teen years.

At the age of seven, I participated in my first communion, dressed in white and surrounded by friends of the same age who participated in this special event. It was at this service that our parish priest asked, "How many of you boys are going to become a priest?" I raised my hand, along with others, in the affirmative. That commitment would shape my life for years to come as a youth and young adult. Several of these early classmates became Catholic priests; one is now a Catholic bishop.

When I was eight, I began practicing to be an altar boy for the Sunday worship service called the mass. I recall Grandma Rose tutoring me in the living room of our home, east of Bridgeport. I went through all of the steps and responses appropriate for the service, including the memorization of the Latin. I actually launched my religious vocation as a nine-year-old boy while serving mass for services in Brewster. Once a young man learned how to be an altar boy, he could be invited to "serve a mass" anywhere in the church. I performed this service from age nine until age twenty-one, virtually every Sunday of my life during that time. A number of Jesuit priests became our close friends while I was serving mass in the Catholic Church. In fact, the priests were frequent visitors to our home on Sunday afternoon for chicken dinner, and they sometimes came for pheasant hunts in the fall. My brothers, Don and Jerry, were faithful altar boys also, and on special occasions all three of us could be found representing our family at significant events in the church.

To be an altar boy, one had to arrive early and leave late to participate in serving mass. We prepared the altar, lit the candles, assisted the priest with the vestments he wore for mass, and helped place the scriptures at the side of the altar. When mass was over, we helped put away the items associated with the service, and the vestments the priest wore were carefully placed in special drawers. We also helped pass the bread for communion. It was quite an honor to be an altar boy.

We Coleman children, including my sisters Kay and Rozella, also participated in regular religious training, called catechism classes. I remember well the summer-school lessons with the Catholic nuns as teachers. This was usually a one- or two-week course of more intense study and activity. The nuns were wonderful and caring instructors. One of my teachers for these two-week religious educational experiences gave me the following certificate at the completion of each year of my attendance:

> This certifies that Gary Coleman has been a well behaved and diligent pupil at the Religious Vacation School and is entitled to this diploma. May you always be a true and loyal CATHOLIC.
> Given this 18th day of June 1949, at Sacred Heart Church, Brewster, Washington.

The following instructions were also attached to the certificate:

The child Jesus is your model. Be respectful and obedient to elders; gentle and kind to all. Keep good company. God sees you everywhere. Read good books. (Most comics are trash, even sinful.) Attend class "A" shows only. Say prayers morning and night. Be at Mass every Sunday. Receive Holy Communion often. Be the pride of your parents, your church and your school. God bless you always!

At age ten I was confirmed a member of the church in a special ceremony conducted by the bishop of the Yakima, Washington, diocese who came to our little town. This was a significant event in the lives of many of us throughout the region. It was on this occasion that the bishop said to me privately, "Gary, someday you will become a priest. In fact, someday you will become a bishop." Our family was named the Catholic Family of the Year, and that was a great honor among our parishioners. As a young adult, following high school, my brother Jerry was the president of the Catholic Youth Organization for one year. We were not idle, during our youthful years, as adherents to our faith. We were taught by our parents to be active members of the church and to lead righteous lives, a foundation that has remained with me.

PROSPECTIVE MEMBERS COME WITH RELIGIOUS,

SOCIAL, AND BEHAVIORAL TRADITIONS THAT CAN

AFFECT THEIR CONVERSION PROCESS.

Like me, many converts are faced with previous traditions that can either be stumbling blocks or stepping stones in the search for truth. The prophet Nephi begins the Book of Mormon with these words: "I, Nephi, having been born of goodly parents, therefore I was taught somewhat in all the learning of my father" (1 Nephi 1:1). We are all deeply influenced by the teachings and traditions of our fathers and mothers and families. Many who are in the Church or out of the Church have had experiences that have led us to say with Nephi that we too were born of goodly parents. Therefore, how do we begin to help others overcome the traditions that keep them from the truths of the restored gospel of Jesus Christ? What can we, who follow the living Christ and His prophets and apostles, do to help our family, friends, and associates "not . . . believe in incorrect traditions"? (Alma 3:8). What can we do for others who "because of the traditions of their fathers" (Mosiah 1:5) are content to live their lives without the benefit of the restoration of the doctrines of Christ for salvation and eternal life? The answer: Teach the truth. Our Father in Heaven loves all of His children. We are all enabled to return to His presence through the ordinances of salvation administered by true servants of Jesus Christ. This process is called conversion to The Church of Jesus Christ of Latter-day Saints. It is this process of bringing people to the restored gospel of Jesus Christ that we are going to explore in this book.

I am one who has been converted to the marvelous events of the Restoration, and most of all to the true teachings of our Lord and Savior. I have been taught in the ways of the prophets and apostles of the latter days. This has brought me out of the limited light of my fathers and into the glories of the beautiful and fulfilling light of the Restoration. This enlightenment is possible for all of our investigator friends.

However, in order to accomplish this task, we must understand the spiritual foundation our friends and neighbors already have. Then, as our circle of love and concern for prospective members widens and we help them overcome the traditions that may hold them back from the truth, baptisms will surely follow. The day will come when we will sit at the water's edge with one of our friends or receive a cherished letter from those we fellow-shipped and in it will be penned the words, "Thank you for helping me find the truth." We long for the day when we will have the thrill of answering that great question, "What must I do to become a member of your church?" If we focus our attitude upon understanding the overall spiritual development of the prospective member, as well as sharing the truth, we will succeed, and we will see the Lord help us accomplish the "thing which he commandeth" (1 Nephi 3:7). This was the case with a family in Duarte, California.

I was serving as the mission president of the California Arcadia Mission. It was a late-night appointment, but the missionaries insisted that a family in Duarte, California, wanted to ask me questions about my conversion. The Finlays asked how I felt about leaving my former church because they, too, were making a great change in their lives to leave their church. It was a beautiful hour together, and they were assured that their struggle was known of God and that He would help them make the correct decisions. My heart filled to overflowing at this opportunity. I testified of my profound gratitude for the Book of Mormon, the key to my conversion. I shared my feelings of abandonment from having left my former faith. I could truly feel their concerns over breaking away from family ties and traditions, and over the kind of commitment their decision would require. This family of four was baptized shortly after that visit. They had been shown the truth and were committed to overcoming the barriers that often come with deciding to be baptized. In order to remain anchored in the gospel, they were given support in their efforts to make such a major change in their lives. The whole ward, led by their special friends, the Reeves, stepped forward and took this family into their hearts. Many opportunities to serve others were opened to them. The father of this family now serves as the bishop in the same ward they lived in when they were baptized. Their spiritual foundations served as a stepping stone as they sought the truth.

I believe that the Lord will help us become more personally involved in understanding and appreciating the previous religious experiences of prospective members as we help them fully come unto Christ. Members can become agents of the Lord in bringing about His purposes. I know we can assist others in these matters.

A man from Russia who had been in the Armenian Orthodox Church for more than ten years was found by our missionaries in California and overcame the traditions of his fathers that had extended for many generations. We met with him on several occasions, and our friendship grew as brothers in the sharing of our conversion struggles. He resonated warmly to principles of the Restoration, in particular priesthood authority and latter-day revelation. As missionaries, we shared with him the beautiful, restored truths of the Book of Mormon and discussed how they deepen our understanding of the doctrines of Christ. His baptism was met with elation in the Latter-day Saint community. He called us when he was ordained to the Aaronic Priesthood, again at his Melchizedek Priesthood ordination, and of course when entering the temple for his sacred covenants. I was thrilled with his goal to bring the gospel to others of his former faith. How dearly I regard this man for his courage to accept the restored gospel after being deeply entrenched in previous religious traditions.

The experience of Amulek in the Book of Mormon is another illustration of a change of attitude and then a change of heart. Amulek had a humbling experience with the prophet Alma that brought a great change in his character. We read of his testifying with great power of the truthfulness of the gospel message and the words of the prophet (Alma 10:10–12). Amulek said that he had hardened his heart many times and would not hear the call of the prophet to help others overcome their false religious traditions, yet he changed his attitude. He said he lived in rebellion against God and would not accept his duties as a member of the Church, yet he repented. It was such a life-changing experience that he even cites the day, month, and year of his change of heart (Alma 10:6). Amulek was able to throw off the traditions of neglect in his service to God. We note that Amulek then lengthened his stride as the companion of a prophet of God and was soon preaching the gospel with great power and authority (Alma 11:46).

The Book of Mormon teaches that we must ever be on the alert for those precious moments when the true plan of God can be shared. I testify that this work is a labor of joy. I certify this is the work of the Lord and that He will assist us as we seek His guidance. There is power in the sweet doctrines of Christ, power to bring others to the restored truths and true changes in behavior. There is power in helping others overcome the traditions of their fathers that have kept them from the true and living Christ. Nephi said, "How is it that ye have forgotten that the Lord is able to do all things according to his will, for the children of men, if it so be that they exercise faith in him? Wherefore, let us be faithful to him" (1 Nephi 7:12).

Nephi's counsel to his brothers is appropriate for our friends and associates. We see that our efforts to help them know who they really are in the overall plan of God will be fulfilled. "They . . . [shall] come to the knowledge . . . of their Redeemer and the very points of his doctrine, that they may know how to come unto him and be saved" (1 Nephi 15:14).

What an awesome responsibility it is for us to bring these precious truths to our brothers and sisters who live beside us and walk the same paths we walk. We can help them build on the traditions of truth that they have been practicing and throw off traditions that keep them from salvation in the kingdom of God.

We can help others add upon their righteous beliefs and behaviors as they come to a knowledge of the fullness of the restored gospel. My parents taught me to be religiously minded, and I appreciate and applaud them for their diligent efforts to help us children stay faithful. The spiritual foundation they helped me establish was pivotal in my search for truth. Many converts feel this way about the role of their religious foundations. By building upon the positive aspects of their previous teachings, prospective members can have the strength to take the next steps of further enlightenment, accept the fullness of the gospel, and develop sure foundations that will keep them anchored in Jesus Christ.

2

AWAKENING TO
RIGHT AND WRONG

When I was in my early teens I participated faithfully in my religious duties. We were strict adherents to the daily practice of "saying the rosary" before retiring to bed each evening. We would kneel on the wooden floor of the living room and recite the memorized prayers in unison, passing our fingers along the rosary beads from one prayer to another. This recital usually took twenty to twenty-five minutes and seemed incredibly long on some nights after a full day of work or school activities. However, we lived by the motto "A family that prays together, stays together." The rosary was our manner of regular family prayer. This was a religious discipline that kept us humble and prayerful before the Lord. It was also a common practice for me to recite these rote prayers, including the Lord's Prayer from the New Testament, as deemed necessary during our private moments of worship.

We children participated in a lot of activities together on the old farm of our youth. As the oldest child in the family, awakening to the responsibilities of making right and wrong decisions weighed upon me. We had the usual experiences of growing up and growing wiser along the way, sometimes at the risk of being foolish and harmful to others. I think experiences with fire were the ones that affected my life the most strongly. Living on a farm with little water available was frightening when a big, ominous cloud of smoke from a grassland or wheat-field fire would appear on the horizon. My stomach would go into a knot at the very sight of such a monster. I suppose I was conditioned to this response because of my own foolishness on a bright and boring summer afternoon with my brothers and sisters.

We were all happily playing with fire along the banks of the creek behind the chicken house, lighting long rye-grass stems and dangling them in the water, failing totally to heed my parents' warnings. Everything was going fine until we pushed our luck too far and accidentally lit the bone-dry grass on the other side of the creek. No problem! Just hustle over to the other side and stamp the fire out! Unfortunately, the fire was up the bank and moving with the wind in seconds. We all were horrified. We frantically beat at the flames with wet gunnysacks, threw shovelfuls of dirt, and stamped on the hungry fire with our pitiful little shoes. Even Mom was enlisted to chase this dragon.

The cloud of smoke rose high, and the wind blew the blaze eastward through our ball field into the ever-present dry grass and sagebrush near our wheat field. We were going crazy. People started arriving at our place by the dozens. Neighbors came in pickups with tank loads of water. Some of the men were using hand-pumped backpacks. Men and women wielded shovels to attack the growing and fast-moving fire. The driveway filled with cars, trucks, and jeeps. The column of smoke rose hundreds of feet, and still the beast marched onward to the Hunt property and fences. Would it ever stop? It was so awful, so frightening, so consuming. After forty acres had been burned, our neighbors conquered the frightening menace. We five children cowered around the yard and watched as our friends and local farmers retreated to their vehicles and drove back down the dusty road to their homes.

It was over, but we dreaded the fact that Dad would know of our irresponsible behavior.

He had been in Omak, fifty miles away, when he saw the smoke. He rushed home, wondering how close the fire was to his home, fields, and family. It was close, very close. His own adventurous children had nearly cost him everything he owned. He drove into the yard as the last firefighter departed down the hill. He spoke not a word. The visual aid was graphically displayed up the hillside and out of sight to the east. He could see where it started—right there within a hundred feet of the house. He knew. Nobody had to tell him.

Dad then did something that will be etched in my memory forever. After gathering all of us into the kitchen, he placed a ten-gallon tub in the middle of the floor and filled it with water. He gave each of us a box of stick matches—a *big* box of matches. He then said, "You may now light each match, let it burn as long as possible, and drop it into the water. Good night." We sat there through the long night, lighting one match at a time until the assignment was completed. I often felt a huge knot in my stomach thereafter when I saw the big smoke burning over the horizon. I never wanted to misuse matches and fire again. I knew it was right to honor my parents and their counsel. I knew it was wrong to be careless about harming other people's property and tranquillity. That fateful day had reinforced my knowledge of right and wrong in a tragic way.

This awakening to right and wrong manifested itself in another way also. In my maturing there began to be the need to resolve serious religious issues in my mind. Some of my friends had entered the seminary for training in religious vocations. I was sharing my faith with others, and they were being led to join in my religious beliefs. But I was troubled by the fact that priests could not marry. I reasoned that if marriage was ordained of God, and I believed it was, how could it be wrong to be married if a man was ordained to the priesthood? Somewhere deep in my being I felt it was right to raise an honorable family. That idea seemed to haunt me each time I pondered going to the seminary to become a priest. Some of the other doctrines of my faith did not seem to square with my scripture study. I was confused about the Trinity and the definition of God and Jesus and the Holy Spirit, yet I did not challenge the authority of my leaders. I tried to have more faith and belief in the mission of the church. My questions heightened and became more meaningful as I passed through certain experiences in my life.

One night I came very close to experiencing death with my teammates as we traveled home from a high school basketball game. The travel in the old school bus to and from the games was always long and tedious, especially after the away games, as we would often arrive home after midnight. One particularly frightening experience occurred on the way home from Leavenworth on a cold and snowy night. Just out of Chelan, heading east on the old road toward Rocky Reach Dam, we were just barely creeping along because of the icy conditions. No sanding of the highway had been done yet. We came to the "super curve" one thousand feet above the Columbia River. Glenn Wiese, who later became my brother-in-law, was driving, and another coach was riding up front with him. We stopped while they debated over staying on the upper side, the wrong side of the road, to get across the deep "super." Our other choice was to go to the lower side that had only a three-foot guardrail between a vehicle and the black hole hundreds of feet down to the rocks and river. Having decided on the upper side, we inched forward, all of us holding our breath. Suddenly the bus began sliding to the right and downward and slammed into the guardrail! We stopped again while the coaches discussed our plight. I was now sitting by the lower side window! It was not a pleasant moment, and I was not happy to be there. We all moved to the upper side of the bus and started forward again, scraping along the guardrail until the bus could be driven away from this life-saving barrier and travel on the flatter surface beyond the steep, sloping curve. It was a long night, to say the least, and we were all praying to get through the scary experience. My questions about life and purpose and direction were heightened. Was I making the kind of choices in my life to merit this protection? These wrestlings with right and wrong, good and bad, true and false continued through my teenage years, shaping and guiding my actions and behaviors until I faced the ultimate choice of my life: the choice to accept the truth of the restored gospel. My experiences of developing my understanding of right and wrong prepared me to see the rightness of the gospel and to have the courage to make the right choice.

PROSPECTIVE MEMBERS ARE TAUGHT
ABOUT MAKING MORAL CHOICES BETWEEN
RIGHT AND WRONG, TRUTH AND ERROR—
EVEN CHOOSING THE ULTIMATE TRUTH
OF THE GOSPEL OF JESUS CHRIST.

We may not know of the ways a person has been taught by the Spirit and awakened to the difference between right and wrong. However, we see the fruits of this teaching when he or she makes the choice to accept the full truth of the gospel. This kind of spiritual awakening to right and wrong occurs in the life of many converts.

Nancy was raised in a devout Methodist family. She became uncomfortable with some issues as a teen and fell away, but from then on she searched for which church she should join. As a young wife she took the lessons of the Catholic Church because her husband was from a strong Italian Catholic family and she wanted to share his religion with him.

At this time, Nancy was also expecting their first daughter. She had felt the spirit of her child with her at times and had strong feelings about the divine origin of a new baby. During a group lesson, she heard of the Catholic doctrine that children are born in sin and cannot be saved except through baptism. She was very disturbed by this idea. She knew that it could not be true. Not only did she feel the sanctity of her unborn child, but she had also lost a sister in infancy years before. Nancy told the group during the lesson that she could not believe this doctrine because she knew that little children were innocent. She told them she would not be returning to the lessons.

Months passed, and when her second daughter was born, Nancy was given further spiritual awakening as she looked at her new baby girl. She said, "Welcome to the world," knowing full well, in her heart, that baby Catherine had come from heaven, but not being able to explain how she knew this. Nancy eventually separated from her first husband, her refusal to join the Catholic Church a factor in the decision. As the religion question still plagued her, she would kneel in prayer with her tiny daughters every night, asking the Lord to help her find the right church for them.

Nancy stayed home from work one day, and two sister missionaries knocked on her door. She saw their sweet faces and wondered if they needed something. They talked with her, gave her a Book of Mormon, and invited her to church. Nancy felt the Spirit that first day at church, and she began taking the discussions.

During one lesson, the missionaries asked her what she thought happened to us in regard to our birth. Nancy responded from her heart, "I believe we came from heaven. I believe we are here to prove ourselves and to be tested. Then we get to go back there." The missionaries were delighted at her answer, wondering how she already knew these truths. This was the plan of salvation. Nancy knew it because she had been given spiritual promptings about the answers to questions she sought. She didn't necessarily know how she had come to her belief, but when the entire plan of salvation was outlined to her, the truth resonated. It was what she had always felt was true, and now she had found a church that taught it as doctrine. Nancy had been awakened to right and wrong, truth and error, long before she joined the Church. This spiritual foundation led her to seek and eventually embrace the restored gospel.

One morning, many years after my own baptism, I asked the Lord to help me find someone who could be introduced to the gospel. As I worked at the LDS Institute of Religion office all day, it was unusual for someone who was not a member of the Church to come and see me. Leaving the office, I thought about my earlier prayer and realized that I certainly had not been proactive in finding someone to visit with. While opening the car door, I noticed a young man standing by the fence some one hundred feet away. I hesitated and thought of my prayer again. The test of my faith was under way! Had the Lord raised up this person for me to meet, or was this just a coincidence? The moment came down to this: "Will you take a step of faith right now?" I have learned to pay attention to what some call "a divine rendezvous."

Closing the door of the car, I walked up to the young man and introduced myself. He was friendly, easy to talk to, and a long way from home. He was a laborer on the remodeling project at the LDS Institute building where I worked. He was working there previous to entering Utah State University on an athletic scholarship. Was he a member of the LDS Church? No. Did he know any members of the Church back in Arizona? Yes. Where were these Mormon friends now? They were on missions. Would he like to meet some of my college-age Mormon friends who attended the Institute of Religion? Yes. Jason joined me for lunch at the institute the following day and met many of my young LDS friends.

In a few weeks Jason moved to Logan, Utah, to begin his university life. His institute director was alerted about this new student on campus. It was reported that Jason had been located and that he was living in one of the university dorms with returned missionaries as roommates. It wasn't long before he called and invited me to his baptism. One year later he called again to invite me to his farewell preceding his mission. What a wonderful member! We have met his family and are so grateful for their progress in the Church. I know this is a work of helping our associates make important choices. Jason had made a choice. In fact, he had made a series of choices. He chose to listen to the message of the gospel. He awakened to principles of right and wrong and chose to seek the truth. He chose to commit himself to that same truth.

The Book of Mormon plainly depicts this concept of being able to choose right from wrong: "Men are free according to the flesh; and all things are given them which are expedient unto man. And they are free to choose liberty and eternal life, through the great Mediator of all men, or to choose captivity and death, according to the captivity and power of the devil; for he seeketh that all men might be miserable like unto himself" (2 Nephi 2:27). We are all given this choice upon entering mortality.

Some Church members feel that people who have not been baptized and given the gift of the Holy Ghost are not taught by the Spirit. This is simply not true. The Lord said in 1829, before the Church was organized, "Put your trust in that Spirit which leadeth to do good—yea, to do justly, to walk humbly, to judge righteously; and this is my Spirit" (D&C 11:12). The promptings of the Spirit are what lead a person to accept the truths of the gospel. The Spirit awakens them to the difference between right and wrong, and it is what teaches them answers to questions they did not previously know. Many of our friends and neighbors receive lessons from the Spirit before they ever hear about our church. This is because the Lord loves all of His children and wants them all to know His plan of happiness. We cannot discount the teachings of the Spirit that occur in the lives of others. These teachings are meant to guide, heal, and bring comfort. What a beautiful aid the Spirit is in our lives. How wonderful it is to help prospective members come to the waters of baptism. Soon thereafter they will be given the gift of the Holy Ghost. Then they will better understand the spiritual impressions they have had throughout their lives, and they will feel the joy that comes from the gift of the Holy Ghost as a constant companion.

Many of us feel that the more overt or forward approach I used with Jason in sharing the gospel is just not our style. We see and hear of aggressive contacts people make with prospective members, but we hesitate to incorporate those methods in our own approach. Let's face it, some of us just don't feel we have the personality or the assertiveness to be quite so open with others about the gospel plan. So, what can the faithful and happy members of the Church do to be involved? We need not go through life feeling unfulfilled in this portion of the Lord's work. There are many worthwhile contributions and gifts we can offer to help our associates understand the choice that is available through the gospel.

We can make ourselves available to invite prospective members into our homes or take them to Church activities or meetings and be wonderful member missionaries. Can't we merely visit people in their front yard, at the store, while watching a ball game, or while out for a walk and feel we are doing missionary work? Of course we can. Many gospel themes can be brought into our everyday conversations. Consider these simple things that can involve each of us in helping others feel an awakening to the truths of God. Activities like these will help us overcome personal fears about the conversion process and help us fellowship our friends and neighbors.

Woven into the Book of Mormon are accounts of people to

whom the Lord's love was clearly manifest through caring associates who blessed their lives by sharing the gospel with them, giving them the choice to come unto Christ. Such a case is the moving account of the rebellious Zeezrom, who was brought to a change of heart and repentance of his anti-Christ attitude through the power of the gospel. Though sick with a burning fever and the tribulations of his errant ways, he "began to take courage" (Alma 15:4) as he was prompted to seek the teachers of the gospel of Jesus Christ. He afterward joined the ranks of the faithful missionaries and preached the simple, saving doctrines of the word of God (Alma 31:6). What a choice he made between right and wrong! He was certainly awakened to the knowledge of the gospel and chose to live a life of righteousness.

We can all pray that the doors of people in our wards or branches will be opened to the gospel, that hearts will be softened, prepared, and changed. *Pray* for the missionaries to have success and to be guided to the honest in heart. *Pray* for guidance in selecting a family to work with; then select one and begin making special fellowshipping contacts with them. May I illustrate the powerful awakening to God's plan that occurred in my doctor friend whose wife was a new member of the Church.

My wife, Judy, and I became acquainted with this couple through activities and socials with members. Early in April, a stake president and I visited their home at the request of the man's wife, who said she had been praying for someone to help her husband. The doctor chose to honor his wife's desire to have him learn more about the gospel. He was very open to our discussion. He made arrangements for the missionaries to visit three times in the following week. His decision to learn about the gospel was most welcome.

He invited the missionaries to visit their home many times and opened his heart to the opportunities the gospel offers. The doctor then asked us to participate in his baptism in mid-April.

The following week he was ordained, received a calling in the stake with his wife, and moved forward beautifully in the gospel. We shall never forget the Lord's hand in helping him with his decision to embrace the truth. Several months after the baptism, the doctor was invited to say a prayer at a special fireside. He responded, "I cannot be at the fireside that evening, President. I am going to be with my wife at our first temple preparation class." This man, who had been educated in higher schools of learning, had now chosen to pursue greater knowledge and blessings available in the temple. The prayers of his wife had been answered. My faith was strengthened by his desire to do what was right for his family and act upon his awakenings to the truth.

Another way we can offer prospective members the opportunity to choose the truth of the gospel is to be more *kind,* more *courteous,* and more *aware* of those who live within the boundaries of our influence. In one ward, members welcome newcomers who move into the ward—members or not—and make them feel at home. This type of fellowshipping creates wonderful attitudes about how to reach out to others and how to be friendly toward new neighbors. It also presents our neighbors with the chance to know the truth of the gospel.

Along with prayer and fellowshipping, we can let the *love of Christ* extend into all our associations. We can watch for opportunities to be helpful to the children, the teenagers, the aged, the sick, the shut-in, and the mothers and fathers who are our neighbors. We can visit the sick, visit with young couples, give attention to toddlers, and share flowers or garden produce with neighbors we are acquainted with on our block. This member missionary principle is shown in the example of a Church member named Karen. Imagine the surprise of Karen's new neighbor, Catherine, as Karen ran by her home in her jogging suit and left her a small gift and a special greeting! Catherine was deeply touched. As subsequent visits continued to produce the same warm feeling inside, she recognized the truth of the gospel and made the choice to be baptized. What joy followed this courageous choice!

What else can we do to develop long-lasting relationships with neighbors? We should strive to be more *tolerant* of the beliefs, customs, and habits of others. Through this attitude we will be more accepting and more willing to share, to listen, and to demonstrate our faith. Understanding and tolerance will move us further along the road of missionary work than any other attitude. It is a Christ-like love that touches the hearts of our friends and neighbors. We must be more tolerant and understanding.

Also, on fast Sunday we can, among other things, specifically *fast* for the gospel to be taken to people in our area and for the Lord to raise up a family to introduce to the gospel. A young couple sought the Lord's help in this manner. Within a year, another couple of their acquaintance announced that they had made the choice to join the Church.

Along with fasting, we should strive to *live the gospel* and *keep the commandments* so that the Spirit of the Lord will be manifest among us as Latter-day Saints and thus influence our neighbors to be attracted to us. One family had heard that members of our church weren't Christians, but from their own experience they came to the opposite conclusion and sought out the missionaries. This family had clearly been taught right from wrong. They actively sought to make correct choices and were led to the truth of the gospel through the actions of their neighbors.

Elder M. Russell Ballard taught, "Our examples will have a powerful effect on others, making the restored gospel become much more desirable to them. Let us, each one, radiate to others the joy, confidence, love and warmth of being part of the true Church of Christ" ("Beware of False Prophets and False Teachers," *Ensign*, November 1999, 62).

These simple ideas will help us break down our barriers of

fear and increase our participation in meaningful efforts to bring about conversion. Simple, everyday experiences will lend support to helping others find the truth. Through following suggestions such as these, no Church members need to feel that they cannot be helpful in awakening others to right and wrong and to directing them to conversion. My conversion was preceded by an understanding of making choices and being accountable for my decisions. Many prospective members have been similarly taught by the Spirit and have a religious foundation. These awakenings to truth can lead our neighbors to make the ultimate choice to accept the gospel of Jesus Christ. I encourage you to be the means by which this awakening to further light and knowledge occurs, thus finding the joy that comes from bringing the gospel to others.

3

SEEKING TRUTH BUT NOT KNOWING WHERE TO FIND IT

As I matured in faith through my teenage years and tried to live by the teachings of the Catholic Church, I wanted to cast my net of knowledge and application of doctrines in wider circles. I approached my final year in high school as a time to look beyond my little community, school, and friends for a career path and a way to pursue my potential. Still, the religious teachings of my youth were affecting my decisions. What to do, where to go, what to become, and how to prepare were all questions of importance for my future.

One of my high school classmates was a member of the LDS Church. I knew nothing of his religion, nor did I ever ask him about it. He did impress me as a person who knew what he wanted out of life, but I did not relate that to his religious beliefs. I should have, but I couldn't, because in my church it was a grievous or mortal sin to look at or become involved with another religion. Neither he nor I knew, at that time, that he was opening a missionary door just a crack to me. Not being able to freely discuss other religions created a huge dilemma for anyone who had doubts or questions about finding new truths. I did not know that the Lord had said decades before to a latter-day prophet, "There are many yet on the earth among all sects, parties, and denominations, who are blinded by the subtle craftiness of men, whereby they lie in wait to deceive, and who are only kept from the truth because they know not where to find it" (D&C 123:12). It was truly a circumstance of "be wrong if you do and be wrong if you don't." It was this very dilemma that plagued me every step along the way of my entry into the world of the restored gospel. This jumble of ideas, doctrine, and confusion was heightened by an experience I had the summer before my senior year in high school. An event occurred that I thought was truly remarkable, and it was a turning point in my life. This event was the miracle on Malone's farm.

I had been gaining experience in previous summers with large machinery, but now I was going to learn more about the proper use of farm resources. I boarded at the Malone farm on Foster Creek the year I turned sixteen. I would drive my '51 Chevy to Mr. Malone's place on Sunday night and board with his family during the week. He had a big John Deere tractor with rear tires as tall as my head. One day, while driving it down a rutted country road, I put the tractor in high gear and opened the throttle all the way. It was only seconds before I was in danger of crashing this large machine. This time I was able to pull back the throttle and get the raging machine slowed down enough to save my neck—and the man's tractor. Speed must be respected, and I had learned another valuable lesson. The tractor's awesome power was in my hands, and I made the choice to respect the responsibility given to me.

One day, I was working the Malone property several miles east of Mansfield, pulling a large piece of equipment called a rod-weeder. A spring hitch is used when working the ground with a rod-weeder. When the rod slips just under the ground surface, it functions as a thing of beauty to uproot every weed in its path. But when the rod strikes a subsurface rock, the spring-loaded hitch disengages from the tractor drawbar with a big bang! At that point, you stop the tractor, back it up, re-hook the rod-weeder cables to the tractor hitch, and go on your way again. This process happens hundreds of times in the course of a job, especially on rocky ground.

This particular afternoon, however, I made a serious mistake. The hitch had disengaged, and so I backed up to the cables as I had done so many times. Leaving the engine idling, I got down off the tractor seat and attempted to hook up the cables to the tractor. I was about a foot short of getting the hitch close enough to the tractor drawbar. Instead of climbing back up onto the tractor seat, I decided to engage the long clutch lever in reverse from the ground. Reaching between the seat and the fender, I could just barely get my fingers around the base of the clutch. I pulled gently, but at that point on the base of the clutch lever, my leverage was all wrong. I engaged the transmission in reverse, and the tractor came rolling back, pushing me toward the rod-weeder frame. I scrambled and stumbled backward, panicking at what I had so foolishly done. I was certain I would be crushed. I felt the frame of the rod-weeder pressing against the back of my thighs, and the drawbar on the tractor was now at the front of my upper shin. It was at this point that the tractor stopped. It just stopped dead.

I was now draped over the rod-weeder frame on my back. The clutch was disengaged. The tractor idled quietly as it loomed over me, and I knew. I knew, in the middle of that field, that someone knew where I was, even who I was. Someone knew that I needed help beyond my ability, beyond my power, beyond my reach. I lay there sweating, heart pounding, limp with fear, and pondered my situation. How did the tractor stop? Had an angel helped me? Was God aware of my plight? Who knew I was there? A very sober and thankful boy extracted himself from the scene. I sat there a long time thinking about my life and my future and my God. The questions swirled in my mind without answers. I sought the truth about these questions, but I did not know where to find it.

The day would come when I would understand that experience better, when the Lord would help me to know, through an ordained patriarch, that there was a purpose for my life and experience here on earth and much more to learn in this mortal journey. Until that day, however, I continued my ever-increasing search for answers.

In the fall of 1959 I left home for Washington State University in Pullman. I immediately became a member of the Catholic Youth Organization and continued to regularly attend church and serve mass in the local community parish. However, I brought my concerns about becoming a priest with me. Was now the time to enter the seminary? An education in the seminary would have provided college-level training. The curriculum would have brought a religious vocation for the rest of my life. Concerns plagued me. The doctrine of celibacy was the most serious barrier. It just did not seem right to live that way. Though entering the seminary would have been viewed as totally honorable and appropriate in my family and among peers, I could not gain any measure of peace about this career path.

I had dating experiences with both Catholic and non-Catholic young women throughout high school and into college. I remember receiving strong counsel from my religious leaders that interreligious marriages were difficult to sustain, so I leaned toward finding friends and associates of my own faith. But for me there came a point in my experience with the Catholic Church where it was difficult to exercise faith in the teachings of the church fathers. For me, these teachings often conflicted with the scriptures. For instance, by Catholic definition, God was incomprehensible. That never sat well with me, even in my very youthful days. Three Gods in one, yet not three Gods—it was impossible for me to know what that really meant, and it was a terrible strain to reconcile these teachings with the book of John: "And this is life eternal, that they might know thee the only true God, and Jesus Christ, whom thou hast sent" (John 17:3). My efforts to comprehend the simple but traditionally taught concept of God as the Father and Jesus as the Son were thwarted by church teachings despite such scriptures as Simon Peter's declaration: "Thou art the Christ, the Son of the living God" (Matthew 16:16), or, in another version, "And we believe and are sure that thou art that Christ, the Son of the living God" (John 6:69). These were trying times for a young man seeking peace in his religious foundations.

Those first years in the university were troubling as I tried to find my way through an ever-mounting selection of ideas, philosophies, and vocational pursuits. My experiences at mass were becoming unfulfilling, rote, devoid of spirit and fellowship. But what was the alternative? To look elsewhere was a grievous and damnable sin, yet to continue where I was seemed a struggle. The search for truths about my religious beliefs continued.

One of the most troubling questions I had about Catholic doctrine was that of the Godhead. This is a common concern for many prospective members and friends. They want to understand God and Jesus Christ. The Book of Mormon prophets taught the simple truths of the Son of God, answering the questions that so many of our friends and neighbors have about the Savior.

"And he shall be called Jesus Christ, the Son of God, the Father of heaven and earth, the Creator of all things from the beginning; and his mother shall be called Mary" (Mosiah 3:8). The Book of Mormon then goes on to teach about the relationship we have with the Savior when we come to accept the truths found in the gospel: "And now, because of the covenant which ye have made ye shall be called the children of Christ, his sons, and his daughters; for behold, this day he hath spiritually begotten you; for ye say that your hearts are changed through faith on his name; therefore, ye are born of him and have become his sons and his daughters" (Mosiah 5:7). During my high school and early college years, I needed these answers. I searched for these truths just as many of our friends and loved ones search for them.

PROSPECTIVE MEMBERS SEEK ANSWERS
THAT CAN BE FOUND THROUGH THE
RESTORED GOSPEL OF JESUS CHRIST.

Many of our friends also seek for truth but do not know where to find it. The gospel of Jesus Christ is so powerful that it can snatch a person, member or prospective member, from the edge of hopelessness and despair. The Jew, the Gentile, the Catholic, the Protestant, the less-active member, the prospective member—all are children of God, capable of seeking truth and changing to the Lord's way. Throughout the scriptures we have examples of "the mighty change of heart," which illustrates the power of the gospel as a change agent when truth is recognized.

One such example occurred in approximately 148 B.C., when a young man sat in a council of evil men headed by King Noah in the land of Lehi-Nephi. The young man's name was Alma (later known as Alma the Elder). The court of men he mingled with was possibly a group of disbelievers who, under the rule of King Noah, had resorted to great sin and abomination in their priestly practices. Because of the subsequent events in the life of Alma, we may conclude that Alma held the priesthood before he, with others, became party to the activities of King Noah (Joseph Fielding Smith, *Answers to Gospel Questions*, 3:203). We don't know to what extent Alma had apostatized, but we do know from the Book of Mormon record that the first message of the prophet Abinadi did not have much visible effect upon this young man

(Mosiah 11). Then, as the doctrines of Christ taught by a prophet touched Alma's soul, he began to seek the truth.

The record preserves for us a precious account of Alma's change of heart. As we read in Mosiah 17:2, we find that later "he believed the words which Abinadi had spoken." The doctrine Alma heard with an open heart was accepted as truth, and subsequently his life was changed. Alma defended Abinadi and was soon thrust out of the court of Noah, fleeing for his life. The change of heart seemed complete as we read in Mosiah 18:1, "It came to pass that Alma, who had fled from the servants of king Noah, repented of his sins and iniquities, and went about privately among the people, and began to teach the words of Abinadi." Alma received the doctrinal truth from Abinadi. His heart was opened to the truth taught by the prophet, and he gave up all in order to live by these truths.

Bringing converts to Christ in their search for truth is an application of "the mighty change of heart" that may occur doctrinally and socially among our acquaintances. There are many people in the Church today who, like Alma, have left home and family for the gospel. They have found answers to questions as the gospel message rings true to them. The change in their lives has been profound and marvelous but challenging as well. I recall home teaching a family in which the wife was said to be a member and the husband a prospective member. After my companion and I had visited with her husband a number of times, he said that he really didn't understand why we continued to visit their family. "After all," he said, "my wife isn't a member, and if she is, I will leave her right here and now!" Such a disheartening situation is not uncommon for many prospective members and converts. These barriers are the adversary's way of distracting people in their search for the truth of the restored gospel and the opportunities it gives us to change our lives. Our missionary efforts, whatever they may be, are our trials of faith. If we never sufficiently try our faith by speaking to people and becoming a friend, by exploring new possibilities of sharing the gospel, or by walking down the path of faith far enough to spark gospel interest in another person, we do not realize the power of the Lord in missionary work. He will open doors and He will prepare the way. He softens hearts. He prepares and touches hearts in ways we have never thought of. In this respect, the Lord does most of the work. He knows who is ready for the gospel. He will assist these people in their search for answers to their questions about truth, using us as a catalyst in bringing the gospel to them.

As members of The Church of Jesus Christ of Latter-day Saints, we understand the fullness of the gospel and know we can find the answers we seek through modern-day revelation and ancient scripture. Our seeking friends need to know that the Book of Mormon answers questions and changes lives. Because the Book of Mormon is another testament of Jesus Christ, it is filled with the defining doctrines of the great plan of God. Nowhere in sacred writ do we find the purpose of this life so completely revealed. It is the Book of Mormon that over and over again refers to eternal life through following Jesus Christ. This book of scripture has proven in itself to lead the children of God to the Savior and the eternal plan of our Heavenly Father. The Book of Mormon restores the completeness of the doctrine of Christ and provides the answers that our friends and neighbors seek. While presiding over the Church, President Ezra Taft Benson said the following about the Book of Mormon: "It contains the words of Christ, and its great mission is to bring us to Christic. . . . Combined with the . . . Spirit of the Lord, the Book of Mormon is the greatest tool which God has given us to convert the world" ("Of the Most Worth," *New Era*, June 1989, 4). Writing a testimony in the front of a Book of Mormon is an entirely appropriate way to help an associate begin the process of learning new truths. Such testimonies need to be sincere, heartfelt expressions written in a simple, straightforward way. They need not be lengthy or flowery. Perhaps the key is to invite the prospective reader of your testimony to humbly and prayerfully consider the message of the book. Here are several samples of messages you could put into your own words in the book you prepare for a prospective member:

• "We are pleased that you have accepted this book from our family. We have prayerfully read it, and we know it is true. We have found great happiness and peace as we have lived the principles of this scripture and the Bible. Joseph Smith was indeed a prophet. Jesus Christ does live and directs The Church of Jesus Christ of Latter-day Saints. We hope you will sincerely study these things. May you come to know, as we do, the truthfulness of these things." Carefully consider what would be appropriate for you and your family to say in the book you share.

• "Many times our hearts have filled with gratitude to the Lord for bringing forth this special second witness of the divinity of Jesus Christ and His gospel. We are pleased that you would take the time to study and ponder its message. It is true. The events surrounding its coming forth through the Prophet Joseph Smith are powerful evidence that it was translated by the gift and power of God. Please prayerfully consider the words of the ancient prophets penned on these pages. We know that the Book of Mormon is a sacred record for God's people in these latter days." Not using these examples verbatim, write how you honestly feel about the book in your own words.

• "We are honored to share our testimony of the truthfulness of the Book of Mormon with you. It has touched our lives deeply and caused us to carefully search our souls for the meaning of life in these troubled times. We testify with no hesitation that this book, like the Bible, is a sacred witness of the mission of Jesus Christ to this earth. Through our acquaintance with this book, we have also come to know that God lives, that Jesus is His divine

Son, and that the gospel has been restored in these latter days through living prophets. These things are true, and we pray that you may come to this knowledge also." You can adapt any of these brief suggestions to your own needs.

• "My testimony to you is simple. This record of ancient scripture is true. In it you will discover an inspiring account of God's dealings with people of the ancient Americas. Jesus Christ's visit to these people after His resurrection at Jerusalem is profoundly described. The book has come forth in our time to be a second witness of the power of God's work among His faithful people today. Prayerfully read and study its sacred message. As you embrace these teachings, you will open a whole new world of spiritual understanding and conviction for yourself. May God bless you to know the truth of these things as I do." Prayerfully consider how you would word a personal invitation to a friend whom you prepare for your book.

After you have written a heartfelt, personal testimony, the next step is to see that the book gets into the hands of a prospective member, either through your own efforts, through your ward mission leader, through a full-time or ward missionary, or through a friend who would be willing to place the book for you. A person must be given the opportunity to read the Book of Mormon in order to sup from its pages and find answers to questions they seek. Such was the case with the following woman.

She came to my office with a member who was a leader in our church and was seeking counsel about how a Catholic woman could resolve some personal concerns. The counselor had told her of my Catholic background and suggested she visit with me about the matter. Our conversation concluded, and then I recommended she consider and pray about a more long-range solution to her needs. She accepted a Book of Mormon and promised to meet with me later. Days passed, and then she called to visit with me again. Upon her arrival, she said, "I came to see if you could help me learn about the Church." I arranged for the missionaries immediately. She was taught and prepared for baptism in three weeks. Radiant and full of joy, she eagerly sought to enter the kingdom of God. The night of her baptism I called the Castleton family in Ogden, Utah. As she entered the church for the baptismal service, I asked her to speak to Sister Castleton on the phone. Sister Castleton asked, "How are you, and what are you doing at the church today?" Our friend replied in a way that brought unspeakable joy to those of us involved. She said she had read the Book of Mormon that the Castleton family had donated to her through the mission and that she was at the church to be baptized! The truths in the Book of Mormon had led her to the waters of baptism, and the Castleton family's faithfulness in this effort helped make the distribution of this sacred book possible. It was a simple act with a life-changing effect.

Our friends and neighbors need to be given the opportunity to find the answers they seek, and we can be a factor in bringing this about. Members of the Church have been termed the "sleeping giant" of missionary efforts. Should this sleeping giant, the more than eleven million members of the Church, awaken to its full potential, literally millions of people could join the Church every year. This is the vision of our great prophet. This is the sacred objective. President Gordon B. Hinckley has said, "We need again to give this important matter its proper priority. The Lord will bless those who assist in this all-important work" ("Find the Lambs, Feed the Sheep," *Ensign,* May 1999, 104). Will you follow the counsel of the living prophet and give this work its proper priority? As we develop the faith and courage to assist others in the search for truth, we can experience the growth that President Hinckley envisions today. We can reach new spiritual heights. We can partake of the joy that comes as we heed the Lord's counsel concerning missionary work.

I wondered what my purpose in life was that day, many years

ago on Malone's farm. I questioned my place in God's eyes and His plans for me. I yearned for the answers to those questions and sought for truth without knowing where to find it. Through the Lord's plan, those who seek the truth will find it in the restored gospel. I know that questions are answered through the gospel and the Book of Mormon. I know the joy of finally finding the truth after searching for so long. This is the joy for which we seek as we share the beautiful teachings of the Lord with our friends and neighbors.

4

Searching to Find Our Way

My university years were filled with new experiences, friends, and preparation for my future. I think I changed my major and selection of a particular degree to pursue at least four times in those years. I wandered from agricultural engineering to political science to vocational education, finally settling on physical education and psychology in the ranks of professional teaching. During my early college days, my father had become hospitalized, my mother was having a tough time caring for the family, and it was difficult to stay focused on my future. I was tempted to return home and abandon my college pursuit. My financial situation was bleak as well, and I was living from day to day on student jobs at night to supplement my summer income, taking out a student loan each fall to cover tuition and housing expenses. I paid the loans back each summer but sought a new loan faithfully each fall. It was a very uncertain time in my life.

As I continued my search for direction, big questions arose every semester: should I stay, should I quit, should I go somewhere closer to home, should I support the family, and so on. The summer following my sophomore year at Washington State University, I joined a friend in Clarkia, Idaho, as a member of a Forest Service crew in the St. Joe National Forest. My years on the farm brought experiences fighting wildfires and enjoying the great outdoors. This seemed meaningful and well suited for me. One achievement in particular gave this nineteen-year-old some needed confidence.

A few weeks into the job I learned of a fire control school that was to be conducted in a remote part of the forest, and I was anxious to try my hand at that opportunity. After learning many skills about compass reading, firefighting, and general woodsmanship, our final task at the school was to chase a smoke. In other words, the fire control officer started a bonfire deep in the forest, and a group of six smoke chasers were assigned to find it. At fifteen-minute intervals one of the six smoke chasers was let out of a vehicle by the side of a forest road, four miles from the smoke, and then required to hike overland to the smoke as quickly as possible. At the point of our departure from the vehicle, we could see the smoke with the aid of binoculars. Immediately after leaving the road, however, the terrain became so rugged that it would be several miles before we could visually locate the smoke again. Thus we had to call upon our training with the use of the compass and general skills in the woods in order to complete the assignment before dark.

As I planned my route, I picked out certain prominent trees, rocks, or points on the ridgelines and moved toward them. Rather than fighting the brush and thickets of the valleys, I hurried along the more open ridges, departing from the direct route long enough to avoid the obstructions and entanglements of the straight line. We carried full fire packs weighing about thirty pounds, including a Pulaski and a shovel, the handles of which projected out of our packs some eighteen inches above our heads. To my surprise I noted, after a short period of time, that the smoke chasers who had preceded me were floundering away in the midst of brush and thickets while I quickly avoided these traps and skirted them in the more open areas. I saw one of my fellow smoke chasers deep in a patch of brush with his shovel handle catching on a limb with every step. As I picked my way through the forest, I occasionally used game trails and logging roads that helped make the way easier. After several hours I could see the smoke clearly. Apparently I arrived at the fire in record time, and the fire control officer asked me if I was the first chaser to be sent to that fire. I happily assured him that I was the sixth man assigned to his fire and that five men had preceded me. In fact, two of the fellows never did find the fire, and they were found late that night on a mountain road far from their goal! I had used my training in such a way that this was a very rewarding accomplishment for me. As a consequence of this achievement, I was assigned to be the trail crew foreman for the remainder of the summer. That sure beat piling brush with the brush crew.

PROPHETS AND APOSTLES WILL HELP US GUIDE
PROSPECTIVE MEMBERS IN THEIR SEARCH TO
FIND THE WAY TO JESUS CHRIST.

I have drawn upon my experience in the Forest Service time and time again as I found my way into the plan of God through the restored gospel. Years ago I heard a phrase that would guide me all my Church life. "Follow the Brethren," my home teaching companion would counsel as we visited our assigned homes. "Keep your eye on the prophet" was a favorite saying of this mentor in the gospel. I have learned many applications of that experience as I have trusted the servants of the Lord. We can pick out reference points in life to help us work toward our goal. Though we may carry heavy packs in life, the prophets will help us keep ourselves properly oriented, and we will not get lost and discouraged and fail to reach our goal of helping others in their search for the gospel. Though we may trod new ground and the fear of the unknown may seem to close about us even as the tall trees deep in the forest, we can put our trust in such reference points as the prophets, the scriptures, and the programs of the Lord. As we note the clearings and open places along our journey, we can catch our breath and strengthen our resolve to reach our goal. Just as the forest smoke is a constant beacon, sometimes seen but more often not seen, so also are the prophets and the gospel a constant aid and comfort in our journey through life. The Lord has given us prophets to guide us and beckon us to better ourselves and others along the way. Living the gospel will help us stay on ridgelines, where our vision is not cluttered and our ability to share the gospel is enhanced.

Our prospective-member friends can benefit from this doctrine just as much as we can, but they need to know that it is available. The doctrine of living prophets is a new idea to most prospective members. They are aware of biblical prophets and apostles who led people to Christ, and they need to see that we are following the same theme as prophets of old. The idea of living prophets in the latter days is a concept born of the restoration of the gospel. The restoration of the true church of Jesus Christ, the bringing forth of the Book of Mormon, the authority of God to act in His name and as His agents, and the performance of sacred ordinances for time and eternity are brought about through latter-day prophets and apostles. God raises up His servants to administer His work by His authority. This is a position opposite that of men taking unto themselves supposed authority of God and developing their own man-made doctrines to form churches of their own liking. These churches of men perpetuate the errors in their own doctrines. Living prophets, however, are evidence of God's working through men in the latter days even as He worked through ancient prophets to bring forth His word.

We can take this analogy of following the prophets a step further. Not only is this concept of revelation and guidance new and comforting to prospective members, but we as member missionaries should also realize how the counsel of living prophets relates to missionary work. Through the years, prophets have given members of the Church guidance and direction about their role in bringing people unto Christ. Such has been the counsel of President Gordon B. Hinckley: "We must continue to reach out across the world, teaching the gospel at home and abroad. A divine mandate rests heavily upon us. We cannot run from it. We cannot avoid it" ("Look to the Future," *Ensign*, November 1997, 67). Our living prophets and apostles have outlined our responsibilities with missionary work. Now we have a choice. Will we follow the Brethren? Will we keep our eye on the prophets in helping our friends and neighbors find the truth of the restored gospel?

We follow the prophet's counsel when we share the gospel with those around us. Prospective members have been brought into the Church hundreds of different ways. Members participate in helping prospective members when they give the missionaries the name of a friend, relative, or associate, and the missionaries then call upon that person to teach him or her the gospel. When members find and fellowship people for missionaries to teach, missionary work is much more effective. Elder Henry B. Eyring of the Quorum of the Twelve has given counsel about this aspect of helping those who are searching for the truth: "The duty to warn our neighbors falls on all of us who have accepted the covenant of baptism. We are to talk with nonmember friends and relatives about the gospel. Our purpose is to invite them to be taught by the full-time missionaries who are called and set apart to teach. When a person has chosen to accept our invitation to be taught, a 'referral' of great promise has been created, one far more likely to enter the waters of baptism and then to remain faithful" ("A Voice of Warning," *Ensign*, November 1998, 32). Full-time missionaries are resources the Lord has placed in our wards and stakes to assist the members and local priesthood and auxiliary officers to bring converts to Christ and establish the Church in their lives and homes.

The best support system for our full-time missionaries is strong member involvement in the conversion process. Elder Dallin H. Oaks, a member of the Quorum of the Twelve, has said that until members become more effective in sharing the gospel, "these wonderful full-time missionaries—our sons and daughters and our noble associates in the Lord's work—will remain underused in their great assignment to teach the restored gospel of Jesus Christ" ("Sharing the Gospel," *Ensign,* November 2001, 7). Stake and ward councils must help members capture the great potential of these full-time servants of the Lord. Missionary efforts can be correlated regularly through appropriate meetings and opportunities to counsel together about individual needs of investigators and converts. All of us are working to build up the Church as the prophet Alma taught: "And they were called the church of God, or the church of Christ, from that time forward. And it came to pass that whosoever was baptized by the power and authority of God was added to his church" (Mosiah 18:17).

Let me cite an example of an occasion when my wife and I followed the counsel of the prophets to find a "referral of great promise." Our family moved into a new home after months of seeking the situation best suited for our needs. One Sunday afternoon following our relocation, my wife, Judy, and I spent a few hours becoming acquainted with our neighbors. We met two families by introducing ourselves to them and briefly telling them about our family. It was a good experience, and we felt accepted by these neighbors. It was also interesting that as we mentioned to our neighbors that we were members of The Church of Jesus Christ of Latter-day Saints, they responded, "Yes, we know!" Somehow our Church identity preceded us.

One of the families we met was a young couple with four

children close to the ages of our children. Gary and Phyllis were soon to become our very close friends. Just a few days after we met this family, my wife was visiting with Phyllis in their front yard. This was the beginning of a very open relationship. Judy and Phyllis became good friends and shared a great deal of time with each other. It was comfortable for these two women to be in each other's homes. Gary and I also began to share more time together. Soon their family joined our family at church for various family activities.

I asked Gary if he would like his family to learn more about our church and to have our missionaries meet with them. We told Phyllis and Gary that we would attend missionary discussions with them if they wanted us to. Gary agreed to have the missionaries, and I set an appointment for the elders to teach them.

Following the first discussion, I drove the missionaries home. Upon returning to Gary's home to get Judy, he asked if he could talk to me a moment about his family. He then said he would like to start the new year off right. He asked if it would be possible for me to baptize them on New Year's Eve.

That was a wonderful moment. Our new friends had already decided to join the Church! We were thrilled for them and thrilled about our missionary efforts in their behalf. Two months later this family was transferred to another city. What if we hadn't met this fine couple and fellowshipped them during the brief period of time when we lived near each other? This father now serves as a stake president. The children in the family have served missions. What a return on our investment of time on that Sunday afternoon! How vital was that one referral in the missionary effort!

From that experience and the counsel of latter-day apostles and prophets, we had learned that there are great blessings from the Lord when we work with families to teach the gospel. In recent years our inspired leaders have focused on ways to hold successful family missionary meetings. Here are numerous suggestions for your consideration in sharing the gospel:

- Prayerfully select a family.
- Get acquainted.
- Invite them to your home.
- Inform them that you are Latter-day Saints.
- Invite them to a family home evening.
- Share a copy of the Book of Mormon that includes your testimony.
- Share your feelings about a specific principle or doctrine.
- Ask questions to enhance their interest.
- Ask the missionaries to teach them in your home.

We follow the prophets when we use prayer as a fundamental aspect of sharing the gospel with our neighbors and friends. Members have been asked to prayerfully select a family to friendship into the Church each year. A few years ago I joined with the stake priesthood leaders and missionaries to make missionary home visits. The bishop, a missionary, and I were assigned to visit a family in the ward. We prayerfully sought the Lord's help for this sacred visit. The man's wife had joined the Church many years before. Her Catholic husband had never had the discussions, though he was quite supportive of her Church involvement. As we visited with him, there was a sweet spirit of love and acceptance in the room. We prayed again with this kind brother and his wife for strength to be full of faith at this special occasion. We discussed the principles of the gospel and their eternal impact upon him and his wife. At the conclusion I challenged him softly, "Will you hear the discussions from the missionaries?" To my great joy, he accepted the challenge. Over the next three months he worked his way toward baptism. In mid-February, he called and invited me to speak at his baptismal service. What a joyous couple attended the sacred ordinance that Sunday evening! The chapel was filled as friends and Saints all witnessed this glorious event. A seventy-two-year-old man was now beginning a new life with his dear companion. Prayer had been an integral part of the entire missionary process, and the Lord then had a hand in our efforts.

Along with prayer, the prophets have also suggested that we acquaint prospective members with Church social activities so they can see Church members in a relaxed and informal religious setting. A common occurrence in these activities has been to draw attention to the evidence of strong family ties and stability. The family-centered lifestyle of many "prospective members" has led members to approach their friends with the gospel message. "The Family, a Proclamation to the World," published in 1995, is a great missionary tool. I share copies of it with others in my travels. Perhaps one of the most newsworthy activities in the Church has been the family home evening program. This home-based environment is an effective method of attracting families to the teachings of the Church.

A profound worldwide interest in genealogy in recent years has also highlighted the Church's involvement in this family enterprise. Genealogy libraries, conferences, and special activities have served to introduce the Church to many prospective members. Family History Centers are wonderful places to acquaint people with the teachings of our church. Family Search Internet Genealogy Service has been an astounding resource for those interested in family history. This service records millions of inquiries on a daily basis.

In addition to family history, the equally successful www.mormon.org invites participants to learn about the general teachings of the Church and is very user friendly. Another very usable tool is the "pass-along" card. These cards offer a sincere source of information about our church and its teachings, as well as a gift that is available when a recipient follows through. In the year 2000, the First Presidency and Quorum of the Twelve declared their apostolic witness in "The Living Christ." It is their latter-day testimony of the divinity of the Savior. It is a profound announcement of the pure doctrine of Christ and His sacred mission, and it can easily be shared with friends and neighbors. A new Church film surely will be of help to all of us. *Finding Faith in Christ* is now in video and DVD format and has been created to assist members with their responsibilities in sharing the gospel. These Christ-centered messages have been prepared to help our associates understand what we know about the Savior. The overall Church program, with its balanced approach to the religious, physical, and social aspects of life, has been an appealing factor to many. As you can see, there are many ways to introduce the gospel to others. The more you know about a person, the more you will know how to best approach him or her with the gospel. Prayerfully contemplate how you can use the counsel of our leaders to bring the truths of the gospel to others.

We are capable and loveable messengers. We have a message to share with our friends and neighbors that can help them find their way through the hazards of the world and come unto Christ. A key element of this message centers on being able to follow living prophets, a new concept to many prospective members. As they come to know the role of Church leaders in guiding them through the thickets of life, they will find great comfort and direction that they had never before known was available. Prophets stand on the watchtowers of life, guiding us to our eternal goals. Let us keep our eye on the living prophets as we take their challenge to spread the gospel and teach others of the blessings that latter-day prophets can ensure.

5

GOLDEN QUESTIONS

In the fall of 1961, my college junior year, I returned to Pullman, Washington, and lived in a second-floor apartment, closer to campus. One evening, several weeks into the fall semester, I met Judy England. She was a member of the LDS Church, the first young woman of that faith with whom I had become acquainted. Something unusual happened to me. The moment I saw her, I had what I understood to be a spiritual prompting. As clearly as anything I have ever experienced, I was told she would have a part to play in my future.

In my youth, I had never entertained the thought of joining another church. I felt that I belonged to the true church, and I was not seeking any other way of life. Meeting Judy that night and walking across campus together led us to talk and share ideas and backgrounds. I didn't go for a walk with her to learn about her religion, but her religion was a part of her, just as mine was a part of me. She talked about her goals, innocently and in a straightforward manner. I had never heard of the concepts she was sharing: eternal marriage, celestial kingdom, forever families. But those concepts pricked my heart. It was the doctrine of Christ that was being taught. Though my life had a religious foundation, I could not comprehend the impact these new principles would have upon my life if I were to accept them. They seemed to sink deep into my being, stirring the questions and concerns I had about the sanctity of the family.

For years I had considered entering the ministry as a priest, but I had struggled with the doctrine of celibacy, or remaining single. These new beliefs about the family were profound to me. What had this Latter-day Saint woman done? She had helped open my mind to new thoughts. She had taught me truths I had never heard before. In a one-hour walk across campus, I discovered that she had introduced me to ideas that were eternal in nature and deeply meaningful. She had shared with me a few pieces of the gospel plan. My eternal past began to awaken within me, and the struggle of rebirth was underway. Long ago a prophet of the Lord counseled, "By small and simple things are great things brought to pass" (Alma 37:6). Could it really be so clear? Could the answers I sought be so simple?

Despite this new awakening, I continued to cling to my childhood religion. As my college years progressed and I became more independent, I developed my desire to know the truth. I became aware of doubts confronting me about my religious upbringing. Yet when one is a Catholic, one has been taught that the doctrine and principles of the church are not to be meddled with. This placed me in a very insecure position: to question or not to question. Judy, being a Mormon girl, naturally introduced me to her faith, she hoping to convert me and I hoping to convert her. From this point on, religion was to affect my life at every turn. I could not escape from the questions raised in my own mind. Catholicism taught that it was the only true church. The Church of Jesus Christ of Latter-day Saints also claimed to be the only true church. I was entering a time of decisions. Religion was such a strong part of my upbringing that this confrontation could not justifiably be avoided. I had to know the answer, the true answer, and this could only be accomplished through study, prayer, and investigation.

My greatest fear was the consequences of challenging the authority and spiritual power of the Catholic Church. Those who have not witnessed this firsthand probably have no idea of the magnitude of such an endeavor. It is not something to be taken lightly or expect will happen easily. It was one of the most difficult decisions I had ever made.

A few weeks later the YMCA sponsored a meeting on campus where an interesting topic was to be discussed. "Mormon Attitude on Life and Death" was the theme, and the presenter was John M. Madsen, a returned missionary who was active in the LDS Institute of Religion on campus. Strange as it seemed, he was also a classmate of mine in a physics course. I had two new friends, both Latter-day Saints, in a period of two to three weeks. What was going on here? John's presentation was in a Student Union Building lecture room. A nice crowd was present. I know because I paced back and forth in the hallway outside the room for several minutes before I entered. For me to be there was blatant rebellion against my faith. I was choosing to listen to the doctrines of another church, a sin of grave consequences, but what a presentation it was. I learned about the plan of God, our premortal life, mortality, judgment, spirit world, resurrection to differing degrees of glory, and eternal life with God, Jesus, and family. Simplicity, order, and truth stirred my soul. I was feasting upon the word of God in a way I had never known before. I hungered for the truth and answers to my questions. I began to seek out the people and the environment in which I could be taught the things of the Restoration, a new word in my experience. The Latter-day Saints had answers to my questions, all of them. It was a new day, a day of awakening from the traditions of my fathers into a world of truth and light.

HAVING THE COURAGE TO ASK GOLDEN

QUESTIONS CAN LEAD OUR FRIENDS

TO INVESTIGATE THE GOSPEL.

My investigation into the Mormon faith began with two friends, friends who taught me gospel principles through open discussion and gentle questioning. This is often how member-missionary work is done. Simple questions. Simple statements of what we believe. Over the years we have often heard reference to the "golden questions" whenever we discuss bringing converts unto Christ. "What do you know about the Mormon Church?" "Would you like to know more?" These have been popular queries. Are there other questions that may be well suited for our particular personalities and lifestyles? Perhaps there are many members who would be willing to try other approaches that are successful in opening a missionary door. Any question may turn out to be "golden" for any one of us. Some are easier for one person to use than for another. Will you take a simple step of faith and ask some questions of those you know? You might find yourself pleasantly surprised at the answer you get.

I will pose a variety of questions that could lead to a gospel discussion. Your question is a door opener for a gospel visit and a key to an exchange of friendship and concern. I have found that questions can be grouped into broad topics or areas of interest and usefulness. As you learn about people, as you observe their lives and situations, you will be better prepared to seize the opportunity to ask them a simple question that will be meaningful to them. As you have a prayer in your heart about suitable questions for you to share, you will gain faith to use them.

FAMILY SUBJECTS

• Is anyone in your family a member of the LDS Church?

- Do you know of any Latter-day Saint families who live nearby?
- Have our family history resources helped you trace your family name?
- Are you related to an LDS family in town with the same surname?
- What are the teachings in your church concerning the family?
- Are you aware that the Book of Mormon teaches about families?
- Are you going to be with your companion and your children forever?
- How does our Heavenly Father inspire strong family ties?
- What do your apostles and prophets teach about the family?

RELIGIOUS SUBJECTS

- Have you ever visited Temple Square in Salt Lake City?
- Have you ever visited an LDS temple or church?
- Will you go with us to our church activity?
- Have you visited our web site about the LDS Church?
- Do you have apostles in your church?
- How did your church get its name?
- Do you believe Christ organized a church when He was on the earth?
- Would you like to know more about our church?
- Are you aware of the book *Another Testament of Jesus Christ?*
- Is there an LDS church in this community?
- Have you heard about the restoration of the gospel of Jesus Christ?

ACTIVITY-ORIENTED SUBJECTS

- Do you have a family home evening program in your church?

- How do you go about tracking your family ancestry?
- Who does the missionary work in your church?
- What meeting was being held at your church yesterday?
- How do lay people participate in your church? (Men, women.)
- What are your church youth programs like?
- Do you have a program for the younger children in your church?
- How are your church leaders chosen for their positions?
- Do your youth prepare themselves for a mission in the church?
- What do you do about religious education in your church?
- Are there any members of the LDS faith where you work or travel?
- Are you going to watch the LDS Church conference on TV?
- Do you have any literature from the LDS Church?
- May I loan you this reading material and pick it up from you later?
- Did you know the LDS Church is growing rapidly?

For every question we prayerfully think of to ask, there are dozens of possible answers depending on the varied responses of each individual. Make a concerted effort to understand the beliefs and concerns of your friends without judging them. With a prayer in your heart, you will enjoy peace about the matter. Perhaps we will be asked questions in response to our questions. If so, the door is open for conversation, for sharing. Often the door will open clearly and easily to a special need you can meet. On other occasions, your question will solicit no response or interest at all. Don't be disturbed about that; maybe the person you spoke to just wasn't in the mood to visit. It doesn't take long to get a feeling about pursuing the matter or dropping it. Whatever the case, you have learned more about what feels best for you in these situations. Most of the time you will find that people are willing to talk and visit with you. Just like members missionaries, the prophets of the Book of Mormon were prone to ask questions. Hundreds of questions dot the pages of this great book. Alma the Younger asks forty-two questions in the fifth chapter of Alma, deep and searching questions about life, death, salvation, mercy, prophets, change of heart, faith, and on and on.

A king mentioned in the Book of Mormon was persuaded to ask how he could learn about and achieve the eternal life that Aaron, a faithful missionary, had spoken of. Note this exchange: "After Aaron had expounded these things unto him, the king said: What shall I do that I may have this eternal life of which thou hast spoken? Yea, what shall I do that I may be born of God, having this wicked spirit rooted out of my breast, and receive his Spirit, that I may be filled with joy, that I may not be cast off at the last day? Behold, said he, I will give up all that I possess, yea, I will forsake my kingdom, that I may receive this great joy" (Alma 22:15).

Without a doubt, a family we met responded to the answers that come from preaching the word. My wife and I met a couple at the baptism of their adult son. Our golden question for them was "Will you be our guests at a regional conference of our church?" Judy, our son Kent, and I picked up the wonderful family on that beautiful Sunday, and we enjoyed introducing them to local Church leaders in the region. They were deeply touched by the meeting—their first LDS Church conference as a Catholic family. The missionaries and I began to visit and teach them. The mother asked for baptism late that spring after several visits to their home. Her husband said he was going to be next. What a thrill it was to hear of their progress, which had started with a simple question.

Remember, when you ask a golden question, you will be participating in a sacred opportunity to open gospel doors to our

Heavenly Father's children. The more you learn from these experiences, the closer you will come to being part of a convert's life. Take a step of faith with a golden question and see where it takes you and your friends. It may be just the question they needed you to ask.

6

FELLOWSHIPPING— A LABOR OF LOVE

By the spring of 1962 I was enjoying my major in physical education. I had also begun my second year of varsity baseball for the Washington State University Cougars. Judy's friend John Madsen often visited me during baseball practice and took an interest in me. John was to be a major factor in my early Church-related experiences, and he is still my good friend today. My interest in Judy was increasing, but the topic of religion kept me fearful of developing our relationship. Many of my visits with Judy also revolved around the subject of religion. We were seeing each other frequently at campus social events. Changing religion was not on my agenda. In April 1962, on Easter Sunday, I attended my first LDS service after attending an early morning mass. I was not impressed by the noise, facilities, and movement during the meeting. However, I was fellowshipped very kindly by the members. They were so willing to discuss my questions and concerns, and they were so sure of the gospel plan.

I began associating more with Latter-day Saints and felt of their spirit and warmth for humanity. During the summer of 1962, following the completion of my third year at WSU, I began to read about the beliefs of my new friends. John suggested I read *A Marvelous Work and a Wonder* and *The Articles of Faith* as an introduction to doctrine, principles, and fundamentals of LDS teachings. This literature seemed to fill a great need and led me to become a serious investigator of the Church. At that time I was not able to attend Church meetings because of my job with the Forest Service. But I read the books John gave me, and I still sought answers to my many questions. On one occasion in July, I hitchhiked all night to Pullman, Washington, from my station in Idaho, and, after sleeping a few hours at a friend's home, I changed my clothes, went to mass, and borrowed a car to drive out to the Grange Hall where the Latter-day Saints met for their services. Why did they meet there? Because it would still be a number of years before sufficient growth of the Church in that area would warrant construction of their own meetinghouse near the WSU campus. It was not easy for me to attend any church meeting except my own during my growing-up years. In fact, that explains why I attended mass on Easter Sunday before venturing to the Grange Hall church early that spring. To purposefully set foot in this strange place was a giant step for me in breaking my personal religious traditions.

Having served mass as an altar boy for twelve years and having experienced the priest being the center of attraction at a worship service, I was hardly prepared for the scene at the Pullman Ward. Everyone seemed to participate in some way or other. Presiding officials, conducting officials, participating individuals, prayers, music, speakers, youth talks, class teachers, greeters, men leaders, women leaders, and so on. It was overwhelming to me at first. But I shall never forget the friendliness and warmth with which I was received by this group of strangers.

I remember John and others greeting me in the parking lot with great surprise. I felt their sincerity, love, and desire to include me in their meetings and activities. My experience at mass had often been so quiet and uninclusive of others. Here at the Grange Hall, as a substitute chapel, everything seemed in total chaos. I vividly recall the group dismissing from the sacrament meeting and assembling in the same area for Sunday School classes. They put up cloth screens between the class groups, and I listened to at least four different presentations that morning as they came filtering through from every direction. This was not my accustomed Sunday morning worship experience. But in defense of the circumstances and the upheaval, I was again drawn to the friendship of these happy people. There was a magnetism pulling me into their fellowship and interest. When it was all over, I knew I had stepped into a new and overwhelming social and doctrinal discovery.

It is important to understand the social changes involved with conversion. During my high school years, I'd had no desire to participate in the drinking and smoking habits that were part of the youth scene. My parents smoked heavily, and eventually my mother succumbed to lung cancer. My father gave up smoking in his fifties and walked away from the nicotine habit in an admirable way. In my youth it was evident to me that athletic demands were best served without indulging in such harmful substances. In those days, there was no talk of drug abuse, for there were no drugs! I lettered in four sports in my high school, and the coaches kept a firm hand on the after-school activities of the boys on the athletic teams.

In college the pattern was the same. However, during my summers in the Forest Service I became acquainted with some of the looser habits of the young adult population. It was before departing for my work in the summer of 1962 that my friend John gave me the two books previously mentioned. I had carefully read each chapter of Elder Richards's exploration of a myriad of doctrines, principles, and practices of the people associated with the restored gospel. But I have never forgotten the impact of the chapter called "The Word of Wisdom." I knew the principles in this chapter were true; they fit my lifestyle and beliefs from many years before. I was in a little restaurant in Clarkia, Idaho, on a Saturday night, alone with my thoughts and my future, when I decided that never again would I touch anything that would violate the Lord's code of health. I walked away from that cafe with a new commitment to do what was right concerning my personal health and well-being.

This wasn't necessarily an easy commitment to keep. I became aware that my LDS friends avoided many types of beverages associated with the Word of Wisdom, including alcohol. I stopped using these drinks as I became aware of the principles of health being taught. While I really had not developed a taste for coffee or tea as a youth, I simply eliminated them from my life and never looked back.

In the fall of 1962 I again returned to WSU. Judy had graduated and was teaching in Spokane, Washington. We were getting more serious about each other, and I was determined to conquer the religion question. John invited me to attend his early morning seminary class for high school students in the Pullman area. I accepted his invitation and became even more engaged in the study of religion. He was teaching a course in Church history, and this introduced me to The Church of Jesus Christ of Latter-day Saints in a truly proper way. Some days I wouldn't attend, but the class would pray me back. My young friends were so encouraging and interested in my questions. They were such a faithful example to me of dedication and commitment to their beliefs. I admired their devotion to the gospel.

FELLOWSHIPPING SHOWS PROSPECTIVE
MEMBERS THAT OUR CHURCH IS
CENTERED ON JESUS CHRIST.

Many converts say the reason they investigated the Church was because they knew there was something different about its members. They could feel the love of Christ emanating from those who have come to know Him. They know they are loved by the members of the Church who welcome them into the fold with open arms. Each of us can apply aspects of fellowshipping to our friends and neighbors. All it takes is love and a righteous example.

I know of a doctor's wife who died of cancer, and her member husband said she had been concerned that she had never helped anyone come into the Church. This member doctor resolved that her funeral would be a missionary effort in her memory. He knew that many friends in his profession would come to the funeral, including a couple who were both physicians. I agreed to speak for the purpose that this faithful husband outlined. The plan of salvation was taught to his friends and associates on that special day. Only days following the service, the couple contacted our doctor friend, inquired about the doctrinal messages of the funeral, and expressed their desire to learn more about the teachings of the Church. Missionaries were contacted, discussion were presented, my wife and I visited with them and reassured them, and other members rallied to their needs. This sweet experience was repeated as it has been for decades. The sacred ordinance of baptism was performed for two special people who humbled themselves before the Lord in the prescribed manner. Our doctor friend's departed companion had fulfilled her hope after all. The key is to teach the word of God wherever and whenever possible. The prophet Alma has written: "They did go forth, and began to preach the word of God unto the people, entering into their synagogues, and into their houses; yea, and even they did preach the word in their streets" (Alma 32:1).

A frequently mentioned difficulty associated with sharing the gospel is a lack of self-confidence and a fear that people may think we are forcing ourselves upon them. This lack of self-confidence and fear of man translates into interesting concerns about personal involvement in bringing converts to the restored gospel. Many active Latter-day Saints feel that their testimony of the gospel is strong, yet they also say they have difficulty sharing the gospel with others. Therefore, Church members often feel that they do their missionary work through one major function: being an example. However, Church leaders welcome more involvement from members in a variety of activities. The prophets continue to call upon all members to study the scriptures regularly. A higher rate of personal scripture study often leads to more involvement in sharing the gospel. No doubt those who are reading the scriptures are developing a greater sense of the need to share the gospel with others. They are assured of who they are and what they can accomplish with the Lord's help. President Boyd K. Packer has taught the following about this concept: "The study of the doctrines of the gospel will improve behavior quicker than a study of behavior will change behavior" ("Little Children," *Ensign*, November 1986, 16). As you study and take into your heart the doctrines of the restored gospel, you will have a greater desire to share the gospel.

On Sunday, June 3, 1990, while praying over a particular matter related to a choice family I had been visiting for thirty-five months, I was impressed to invite the father to a special Church program that evening. Leland was a staunch Catholic who honored his wife's LDS Church roots and allowed his children to be raised in and influenced by her church. For twenty years he had accepted assignments in Scouting and other Church programs where he could serve his children as they grew in the gospel. We first met in the early days of my service as a mission president, and as the months went by, we would call each other and visit together, and we even prayed together in his home. All the missionaries assigned to his ward were asked to teach and testify to him month after month. He had friends throughout the community who took an interest in him and his beautiful family. He was included in the activities and projects of the ward and stake family.

Upon arriving home late that morning, I called his wife and assured her that Leland was invited to the program where there would be a special message for him. Much to my delight, he came to the meeting! President James Smith, the stake president, and I challenged him to prepare himself for baptism and set aside the traditions of his fathers that he had been struggling with. In the ensuing two weeks, many people spoke words of faith, love, and testimony to our dear friend. Even as late as Saturday morning, the day before the baptismal service, he had doubts. But after a lengthy home visit, a counselor in the stake presidency received a firm commitment from Leland that he would be baptized. On Father's Day, June 17, in the presence of four former bishops and more than a hundred friends and family members, Leland was baptized. Much rejoicing was witnessed in that stake by all who were present. His son, in the Provo MTC, was notified that his first baptism, though performed by others, was his father. One year later, Leland told me about his sweet experience of attending the temple with his family. Fellowshipping was the key. A continuous outpouring of love over many years softened his heart and led him to the mighty change. How thrilled we are at his continued progress in the gospel as he and his family grow and prosper in callings and service.

How are we going to move ahead in this work? As we begin to pray, fellowship, and actively involve ourselves in helping convert others, thousands of families will benefit. Trusting in the word of the Lord and taking steps of faith will help us overcome real barriers of fear and lack of self-confidence. Will you explore ways to fulfill your missionary responsibility and enjoy more involvement in bringing converts unto Christ? We can share ways of taking these steps with each other that will lessen our fears about missionary experiences. Be yourself. Love others. Show them that they are choice daughters and sons of God through your friendship and your message of the gospel. The Lord will give you courage in this great work of fellowshipping. The Book of Mormon explains the reward available to those who perform this labor of love: "If ye have come to a knowledge of the goodness of God, . . . and also, the atonement which has been prepared from the foundation of the world, that thereby salvation might come to him that should put his trust in the Lord, and should be diligent in keeping his commandments, and continue in the faith even unto the end of his life, I mean the life of the mortal body—I say, that this is the man who receiveth salvation, through the atonement which was prepared from the foundation of the world for all mankind" (Mosiah 4:6–7).

7

COMING UNTO CHRIST THROUGH THE RESTORED GOSPEL

Later in the fall of 1962, and during my participation in the seminary class, I struggled mightily with the issues of restored religion. In fact, my mind could not be freed from the mental turmoil of joining another church. I was carrying sixteen hours of schoolwork, and it was a real test for me to keep a proper focus on my studies. The truths of the restored gospel of Jesus Christ were beginning to be manifest to me. I had been to a stake conference in Spokane, Washington, where Elder Boyd K. Packer had taught the doctrines of the restored gospel. Though I did not know the truth of these things, I knew that he knew the truth of the things he taught. True conversion was not far away.

John's early morning seminary class was introducing me to the defining doctrines of the restored gospel. I was absorbing the doctrine of Christ through the plain and simple teachings of the Book of Mormon and the events of early Church history. I mention the Book of Mormon here because a copy was given to me just days before my decision to join the Church. I don't know who prepared it for me. (I am referring to the practice, years ago, where members of the Church marked a copy of the Book of Mormon for investigators.) My book had the numbers of various verses circled in red pencil with the words "go to page 30" (for example). The marking system focused on the defining doctrines of the restored gospel.

The clear, plain truth about the Godhead—about God the Father, Jesus Christ as His Only Begotten Son, and the Holy Ghost as a testifier and witness of the purposes and plans of the Father and the Son—was clearly illustrated to me. Jesus is the Savior and Redeemer and the only way to salvation and eternal life. Verses were marked referring to the power and authority of God through prophets, apostles, and a holy priesthood. Further, marked verses dealt with principles of faith and repentance and the ordinances of the gospel that lead to eternal life. There was evidence of revelation, inspiration, miracles, and the word of God to man through His appointed servants. There was also the plan. Oh, how I resonated to the plan of salvation, the plan of happiness, the great and eternal plan of God, the plan of mercy, the plan of redemption! The last verses marked in my little blue paperback copy of this testament of Jesus Christ were Moroni 10:3–5, which included these words: "When ye shall receive these things, . . . ask God, the Eternal Father, in the name of Christ, *if these things are not true;* and . . . he will manifest the truth of it unto you, by the power of the Holy Ghost."

ALTHOUGH THE SOCIAL AND DOCTRINAL

CHALLENGES THAT PROSPECTIVE MEMBERS FACE

ARE VERY REAL AND OFTEN DIFFICULT,

CONVERTS FIND HOPE IN THE SAVING

ORDINANCES THAT ACCOMPANY THEIR

DECISION TO ACCEPT THE GOSPEL.

The sequence of events at that point in my life are indelibly etched on my memory, my heart, my mind, and my soul. The following morning, at the seminary class, Brother Madsen introduced us to a recording by President Hugh B. Brown of the Church's First Presidency. I listened carefully and prayerfully. This was a major step for me; letting go of papal and priestly authority was now possible. For months I had learned of Joseph Smith the Prophet. My summer reading had introduced me to him. It was not easy to accept a prophet when I had been taught all my life that a latter-day prophet is a false prophet. The traditions of my church taught that popes and priests represent Christ on the earth and had His authority in a continuous line from the apostles of former days when Christ lived on the earth. In President Brown's "Profile of a Prophet," I still hear, ringing in my ears, his stirring declaration undergirding and overarching all the arguments for or against prophets in the latter-days; Joseph Smith was a prophet of God. I gained a testimony of Joseph Smith the Prophet that very hour. It was a stunning development in my long months of searching for truth. It was such an urgent and overwhelming experience that I could not wait a moment longer to resolve the issue of traditional religion or restored religion. I knew I must resolve the matter of joining the Church or leave it alone once and for all. My studies were suffering since I gave my waking hours to the pondering of religious matters. I had to be so sure in my decision. My example to my family of what religion I chose to live had to be based upon truth, not error. How could I be sure? I resolved to go to the Lord in earnest prayer about my struggle. It was time to do as the prophet Alma had taught when asked by a friend in need of answers: "What shall we do?" The scriptural prompting was, "If ye will awake and arouse your faculties, even to an experiment upon my words, and exercise a particle of faith, yea, even if ye can no more than desire to believe, let this desire work in you, even until ye believe in a manner that ye can give place for a portion of my words" (Alma 32:9, 27).

Immediately I returned to my apartment and poured out my

heart to the Lord—not in the rote prayer of my youth but as a son of God seeking answers to questions. I had read the verses in the tenth chapter of Moroni and decided to apply the words of verses 4 and 5. I did ask God, in the name of Jesus Christ, if the precepts I was studying were true. I asked with a sincere heart, with real intent. More than anything I had ever wanted, I wanted to know what to do about religion. I asked about Joseph Smith. I asked about the restoration of the true church. I asked about the Book of Mormon. I asked about the reality of Jesus Christ and His work. I pleaded with the Lord to reveal to me what I should do.

I received the answer to every one of my questions. By the power of the Holy Ghost, from the top of my head to the soles of my feet, I received the answers. I knew the truth of all the things I pondered. I felt a burning in my whole being that removed every doubt, every fear, every concern. Relief and peace came over me. I knew what I must do. Oh, that I could pen the feelings I felt and the knowledge I gained through this manifestation of spiritual power that morning. I can only declare that I know, by the power of the Holy Ghost, that these things are true. From that time forth, there has never been a doubt. I had never before had such an electrifying experience. I had paid the price to know, in the Lord's way, what to do.

I experienced personally the scriptural promise of the prophet Moroni, the concluding writer in the Book of Mormon. I had asked God in humble and sincere prayer if *these things,* the things I had been pondering for many months, *these things* I had to resolve, *these things* that would take me from false traditions and into the light of the Restoration, were true. Moroni says that God will manifest the truth unto the sincere seeker of *these things.* And God did manifest it. He helped me. He lives. He cares about the son or daughter who asks for help in *these things.* I know, because He cares about me. My faith in Christ was sufficient to merit an answer to my pleadings in the name of Christ. The influence of the Holy Ghost was sent to me about *these things* to allow me to feel that sacred and convincing power in my whole being, undeniably and with full clarity and plainness. I know because I am a witness of the power sent by the Holy Ghost. Was the restored doctrine of the Godhead true? Can there be any doubt as to the reality of *these things* pertaining to the Father, Son, and Holy Ghost? Certainly not to this young man seeking the truth within my small sphere of needs. The Book of Mormon had led me to the plain and precious word of God, and it was having a "more powerful effect" upon my mind than "anything else" that had happened to me. The Book of Mormon, my seminary teacher and class, and latter-day prophets had lead me to "try the virtue of the word of God." What power there is in the restored gospel to effect change in the life of a seeker of truth (Alma 31:5). Moroni's promise was fulfilled for me that morning and has been expanded during my years in the Church.

This was the most profound part of my doctrinal conversion. The churches of men had produced great errors in their teachings about the Godhead. Apostasy was rampant on this subject. However, my spiritual experience that morning made clear to me the true doctrine of God. God answered my prayer through the power of the Holy Ghost because I had exercised faith in Christ.

The restored gospel teachings about the Godhead are plain and precious. They were taught when Jesus appeared to the people of the Book of Mormon in the Americas. We read these precious words from God the Father: "Behold my Beloved Son, in whom I am well pleased, in whom I have glorified my name—hear ye him" (3 Nephi 11:7). In response to His Father, the Son replied, "I am Jesus Christ, whom the prophets testified shall come into the world" (3 Nephi 11:10). Could any declaration be clearer than this? Jesus defines His doctrines and the very points of doctrine needed for salvation in His church and kingdom:

"Behold, verily, verily, I say unto you, I will declare unto you my doctrine" (3 Nephi 11:31). "Verily, verily, I say unto you, that this is my doctrine, and I bear record of it from the Father; and whoso believeth in me believeth in the Father also; and unto him will the Father bear record of me, for he will visit him with fire and with the Holy Ghost. And thus will the Father bear record of me, and the Holy Ghost will bear record unto him of the Father and me; for the Father, and I, and the Holy Ghost are one" (3 Nephi 11:35–36). It is Jesus who defines the doctrines of His gospel— not men, not councils, not opinions and decrees of men, not theological or philosophical pronouncements of men, but the Lord Himself who points the way for true converts to find eternal life in His church and kingdom. This is the message that our prospective members must come to know for themselves. They can, through the same process I did, the same process as outlined by Moroni.

Following my prayer that day in late October, I pondered these things carefully and then left my apartment and rushed back to the little seminary and institute building. I declared to John and Don'L Peterson, the institute director, that I wanted to be baptized. They were shocked. They said I would need the "lessons." I wondered why lessons were necessary as I recalled my sacred and powerful experience moments earlier. They persisted and said I would need the missionary lessons. I agreed that it was necessary to have the discussions. "Where are the missionaries that give these lessons?" I asked. They replied, "We don't know, but we will find out." The discussions were finally set for the next week with two missionaries, the first I had ever met. They taught me the formal missionary discussions and helped me set a baptismal date for November 17, 1962. Though only two weeks away, it seemed a long, long time for me.

In the meantime, I called my mother to share with her my plans to leave the church of my father, mother, and family. It was a time of great sorrow for her, and she wept as with a truly broken heart for her eldest son. How many times I have heard others say in despair, "I can't go against the wishes of my mother. It would break her heart." To her on that day I could only say, again and again, that I knew the Church was true and I was doing the right thing. I had always known that this day of declaration would be one of the most difficult of my life. What a paradox. The first convert in a family must, in essence, leave the family to become the means of serving the family through the ordinances of the temple. Even Jesus counseled two thousand years ago, "I am come to set a man at variance against his father, and the daughter against her mother, and the daughter in law against her mother in law. And a man's foes shall be they of his own household. He that loveth father or mother more than me is not worthy of me: and he that loveth son or daughter more than me is not worthy of me. And he that taketh not his cross, and followeth after me, is not worthy of me. He that findeth his life shall lose it: and he that loseth his life for my sake shall find it" (Matthew 10:35–39). The doctrines were clear. I know of nothing as important as obeying my Heavenly Father and my friend and Savior, Jesus Christ. This was a test right up front, before baptism, before the aiding and sustaining power and influence of the gift of the Holy Ghost—would I follow Jesus? Yes. For I knew the only sure way to eternal life and eternal families was through Him.

The doctrines of faith in the Lord and repentance of my sins and errors of past years were like a sweet, healing balm of comfort and assurance washing over me. These are real feelings of relief and goodness and assurance of doing what is right. Perhaps one approaches, in a small way, this miracle of peace as did Alma the Younger when he said, "My soul was racked with eternal torment; but I am snatched, and my soul is pained no more" (Mosiah 27:29). We are left to say, "Thanks be to God for His mercy unto His children."

My mother thought I was leaving one faith for another because of my increasing attraction to Judy. This was a reasonable concern, but I was determined to continue on the path of total change of my life to bring about this far-reaching conversion to Jesus Christ and His restored church. My mother felt I was lost to a strange and obscure religion of little consequence. Little did she know that my actions would be the eventual means for generations of our family to partake of the ordinances of eternal life. A moment of supposed shattering of family ties would eventually lead to sacred covenants that bind families together for eternities.

My father never did accept my decision and felt I had betrayed him and all he held dear. This was a profoundly lonely time. I felt cut off from the ones I loved and the support system that comes with family ties. Thousands upon thousands of converts go through this heartbreaking struggle as they give their all to the One who will give them a new heart and His name, the name of Jesus Christ. This name makes them new creatures and is required of all who come unto Him with full purpose to follow His example and keep His commandments: "This is the means whereby salvation cometh. And there is none other salvation save this which hath been spoken of; neither are there any conditions whereby man can be saved except the conditions which I have told you" (Mosiah 4:8). My doctrinal and social conversion was gaining momentum, and yet the new birth was also painful. I let go of the past and walked into the light of the gospel. There were many moments of struggle between giving up the old ways and embracing the new ways. It is a very real wrenching of the soul.

I bore my testimony in a small group at the Madsen home, during a gathering called a cottage meeting, the day before I was interviewed for baptism by an elder who was a district leader in the mission. I remember his wonderful demeanor as a servant of the Lord. My friend John Madsen baptized and confirmed me in Moscow, Idaho, some eight miles east of Pullman. My seminary classmates and Judy were in attendance. I had broken away from the traditions of the *church* fathers and *my* fathers. I had done as Jesus had done and as He asks all of us to do in His holy name. That very night as Judy and I returned to her home on a snow-covered and icy highway in eastern Washington, the Lord helped us avoid a serious accident. As two cars collided on a narrow bridge just in front of us, they bounced apart, and I was able to swerve between them as a path seemed to open just in time for us to pass through. The car behind us also crashed into one of the cars on the bridge. We stopped to help the obvious victims, and we paused and thanked God for His kindness once again. Clearly the Lord had His hand in my life and in my decision to come unto Him.

I know God lives and has a divine plan for all of us. Can you see that the path to conversion is, in reality, not an event but a process of multiple changes that occur in our social and doctrinal awakening over a period of time? It goes on and on throughout our lives, even after baptism. We must understand this in order to understand our prospective members. This process of social and doctrinal change does not end with baptism. Baptism is often simply the beginning of the changes. As Nephi said, "Ye must press forward with a steadfastness in Christ, having a perfect brightness of hope, and a love of God and of all men. Wherefore, if ye shall press forward, feasting upon the word of Christ, and endure to the end, behold, thus saith the Father: Ye shall have eternal life" (2 Nephi 31:20). Surely it is a predicament of untold dimensions for the Lord to persuade a new convert to shed incorrect family traditions in order to bring eternal blessings to that same family for generations to come—not only that, but also to be able to bless past generations in that same family. All of this is truly a marvel to behold. The very family ties that become so strained as the convert approaches the new way of life are the same family ties that are carried to the temple over the years to be bound together by eternal ordinances. With my baptism, a modern-day pioneer had begun the long journey to the promised land of a sacred family search that would yet bless untold generations with the restored gospel. The despair that arose through the perceived breaking of family ties as a consequence of my baptism was overcome through faith in the Lord and trust in His teachings.

8

GROWTH AND PROGRESS THROUGH RESPONSIBILITY

It was the Monday after I was baptized a member of The Church of Jesus Christ of Latter-day Saints that I met my younger brother near the campus library. All of the family had fears of my joining the Church, and as I now approached Jerry, I sensed the first defense of my action. "Did you go through with it?" he asked. "Yes," I answered, "I was baptized Saturday night." We stood there looking at each other, searching for words that would be appropriate. "I feel good about what I have done," I said. Then he looked into my eyes and surprised me with his next remark: "You're my oldest brother. I know you wouldn't have done it if you didn't think it was right." A surge of relief flashed through me.

I had been wrestling for months about the impact of my investigation of the Church on my family. Being the oldest son, I was especially sensitive to the role I played in leading my younger brothers and sisters. I had to be sure, absolutely sure, in this matter. The hours, days, and months of mental turmoil are still vivid as I sought the answer to the question "Which church is true?" With a new feeling of peace in my heart, I sought the opportunity to share the truths I had discovered with other members of my family.

Just days after visiting with Jerry, I had the opposite experience with a Catholic priest I had been acquainted with for several years during my college days. I saw him coming up the opposite side of the street on campus. He crossed the street to intercept me on the sidewalk. No greeting, no handshake, no smile or friendliness as in the past, just a theological question in my face. He asked me one serious question about my belief in Jesus Christ, to which I responded in faith. He said, "That's what I thought," then turned on his heels and walked away. I was now a believer and defender of my new way of life. I had made the social and doctrinal break from the past and had set a new course. It was a time of great need for friends in the gospel.

A few days later I was ordained a deacon in the Aaronic Priesthood, and I was serving in my first Church calling. My bishop was wonderful. He had sat down with me and discussed the need to extend to me a calling in the Church. I was stunned and surprised that this responsibility would come so soon. What a blessing it was to begin this nourishing process in the true church where everyone is needed to perform service to God and man. Imagine my trepidation as he stated the call to this twenty-one-year-old newly ordained deacon: "We feel inspired to invite you to serve as an Aaronic Priesthood quorum instructor." He assured me that another man would be with me as a member of the Young Men's presidency and that occasionally a member of the bishopric would sit in on our class to be of help. He gave me the manual of instruction and explained that lessons were prepared on different gospel topics and I would present one each week to the boys in the quorum.

I felt that this was a huge responsibility and way over my head, but I came to realize that this was the Lord's way. I came to church each week, I prepared my lessons, I learned the gospel in order to teach my class, and I was nourished by fellowship, study, prayer, and the doctrines of Christ. I was able to pass the sacrament once a month with my youth and young adult brothers in the priesthood. I was called as a home teacher and received further instructions in the work of the Lord. I was growing and becoming a retained convert. I was eager to move along in my priesthood progress as a teacher, priest, and elder.

I was a priest for two weeks before being ordained an elder. All my life I had thought of being a priest. Now I was a priest in the true church. Because of this I really wanted to bless the sacrament as a priest. I could see I had one Sunday to do so because I was about to leave my ward for the summer to work for the Forest Service. Obtaining a recommend from the bishop to perform an ordinance outside my home ward, I drove to St. Maries, Idaho, the following Saturday, located the local branch of the Church, and checked into a motel. I was awake early Sunday morning and drove to the Church at least an hour early. With my recommend in hand, I sought out the branch president as soon as he drove up to the building. I explained, "I was ordained a priest last Sunday and will be ordained an elder next Sunday. Could I bless the sacrament here in your branch today, President?" He replied so kindly, "You are here at the right time, Brother Coleman. We have no priests in our branch, so you can bless both the bread and the water today." It was a wonderful blessing and honor for me to perform that sacred ordinance one time as a priest holding the Lord's authority. I was thrilled to be part of my new church, new friends, new responsibilities, and new nourishment. I was certainly blessed to have wonderful leaders who gave me the opportunity to serve in meaningful ways as I started my journey into the kingdom of God.

As the school year began that fall, Jerry and I were both attending WSU. He was a sophomore and I was a senior. We both held campus jobs and were able to scrape together enough money each semester to enroll the following semester. Christmas vacation was approaching, and it was evident that there were not sufficient funds for either of us to continue in school unless some extra work was secured. We determined that we could work an extra week and thereby be able to stay in school. I invited Jerry to share my apartment with me since his dorm would be closed for vacation and my roommates would also be going home. As we laid these plans, I kept thinking that perhaps the opportunity to share the gospel with him would become available. Then my plans hit a snag—he would work the night shift and I would work the day shift. We would be together only during breakfast and dinner hours.

How promising those hours became! Each day a new question was presented. Each day he would go visit the Catholic priest and ask him about the principles we had discussed. An interesting thing began to happen. At first the priest didn't take Jerry seriously, and he would come back to the apartment with his questions unanswered. Then the answers that were given could not satisfy Jerry's hunger for the truth. As each day passed, the pace quickened in the search for truth. He was eager to learn, and I was overjoyed at the opportunity to share my newfound love of the gospel with him. This Christmas vacation was turning out to be one of the most satisfying experiences of my life. It was an experience in giving and sharing that I shall never forget. After a week of these discussions and daily checking with his priest, Jerry declared, "I want to join your church. You have the answers to my questions."

Every waking hour was spent at the little table in the kitchen giving and receiving the simple witness that the gospel of Jesus Christ provides. Our meals were almost incidental compared to our feasting on the gospel message. We terminated our employment at the school near the end of December and boarded a bus for the half-day's ride home to be with our family. This trip was the shortest I have ever experienced, though I had traveled those miles many times. The things we shared made the time fly by so quickly. After we arrived at home, not much was said there about the fact that I had joined the Church. The mood of everyone was subdued, as if they were waiting to see what such an experience had done to me. I had a new appreciation for my family as I began to sense my responsibility to live my religion and share the gospel with them as I had been doing with Jerry. The beauties of the teachings of the Church and the profound doctrines of Christ are a foundation that is so helpful in our early days of conversion. I hearken often to the testimony of Helaman as he counseled his sons: "Remember, remember that it is upon the rock of our Redeemer, who is Christ, the Son of God, that ye must build your foundation; that when the devil shall send forth his mighty winds, yea, his shafts in the whirlwind, yea, when all his hail and his mighty storm shall beat upon you, it shall have no power over you to drag you down to the gulf of misery and endless wo, because of the rock upon which ye are built, which is a sure foundation, a foundation whereon if men build they cannot fall" (Helaman 5:12).

Jerry and I returned to school early in January and continued to discover together the beauties of the restored gospel. With his increased association with Latter-day Saints came the decision to join the Church, and he was baptized in March 1963. What a glorious day it was for me! Now I was no longer alone in my separation from the family. We sat down after the baptism and rejoiced with each other about our hopes and concerns for our parents and brothers and sisters. Our bond as brothers in the gospel as well as brothers by mortal birth has been strengthened through each passing year. As a consequence of this great experience of gospel sharing that Christmas, I have never forgotten the impact of the responsibility to set the proper example to others in my family. Now we could grow together in the work of the Lord.

My learning did not stop with my baptism. It continued as I was given the responsibility of a calling to teach in an Aaronic

Priesthood quorum, the responsibilities of blessing the sacrament, and the member missionary responsibility to share the gospel message. This church is not an idle man's church. We grow by being involved. That is the way of the Lord's gospel. I felt so grateful for all those who showed genuine interest in my participation and growth as a new member by offering me ways to be involved in the Church.

CONVERTS NEED A RESPONSIBILITY IN ORDER

TO CONTINUE GROWING IN THE GOSPEL.

President Gordon B. Hinckley has taught that every convert needs three things: a friend, a responsibility, and nourishment in the word of God. He has also spoken of "the urgent and pressing need to fellowship those who join our ranks" ("Converts and Young Men," *Ensign*, May 1997, 47). These four things are beautifully woven together in the growing experience of the new convert and the growing membership of a worldwide church. They all were part of my growth as a new member of the Lord's kingdom here on earth.

This idea of growing in the gospel after conversion is reinforced in the Book of Mormon during the account of Alma and the sons of Mosiah. As they met near Zarahemla, they did "rejoice exceedingly" to see each other again. For many years they had all been laboring in missionary work following their dramatic conversion to the ways of the Lord. Why did they rejoice? Because, as Alma says, "they were still his brethren in the Lord." They wanted to be missionaries and help others experience the power of Jesus Christ in bringing about true conversions. And to make it even better, they "had waxed strong in the knowledge of the truth." And the reason for this strength and joy? "They had searched the scriptures diligently, that they might know the word of God" (Alma 17:2). Further, they had prayed, they had fasted for the success of the work, and they had such great faith that "they had the spirit of prophecy, and the spirit of revelation." This brought them the added blessings and power of teaching, "and when they taught, they taught with power and authority of God" (Alma 17:3). Many of those brought to "believe in their teachings . . . were converted unto the Lord, [and] never did fall away" (Alma 23:6).

Helping converts build a solid foundation in the restored gospel will assist them in "never falling away." In this effort, we cannot underestimate the value of giving new converts the opportunity to serve in the Church. Takuji is a man who joined the Church as a young boy. As a teenager, he purchased a new motorcycle that brought him great joy and freedom. On his way to church one Sunday, he approached a crossroad and was suddenly faced with a choice. A left turn would take him to the church building and a right turn would take him to the beach. It was a beautiful, clear day as Takuji made that right-hand turn toward the ocean for a day of fun on the beach. As a result, he did not return to church for many years.

Four years later, Takuji met the missionaries. They began teaching him the gospel, not knowing that he was already a member. On the third lesson, the elder asked him if he would be baptized. Takuji said, "No." Surprised, the missionaries inquired about his reasoning, because he had sensed Takuji's great interest in their message. Takuji was embarrassed at the response he had to give: "I am already baptized." Thinking that the missionary would rebuke him for his inactivity, he was shocked when this fine elder replied, "That is great. I need your help." Takuji worked with the missionaries, side by side, as they set up a branch in their area. Then, when a singles branch was needed in a different location, Takuji went with the elders to help them establish that one as well.

What a wonderful understanding and insight this missionary had that day. He put Takuji to work, gave him a responsibility, and taught him how to serve in the Church. Takuji went on to marry in the temple, and he and his wife are raising four beautiful children in the gospel. They are known in their ward and stake as members who can be counted on to fulfill their callings with energy and devotion to the Lord. Takuji has affected many lives through the Young Men's program and Scouting, and he is currently serving as both a Gospel Doctrine instructor and a Cub Scout den leader. His wife, Kuniko, is the stake Relief Society president. Their solid testimonies, founded on the restored gospel, are strengthened by their continuous service in the Church that was taught to them so many years ago.

Elder Richard G. Scott has given excellent instruction on the joy of involvement and service: "There are few things in life that bring as much joy as the joy that comes from assisting another to improve his or her life. That joy is increased when those efforts help someone understand the teachings of the Savior and that person decides to obey them, is converted and joins His church. There follows great happiness as that new convert is strengthened during the transition to a new life, is solidly grounded in truth and obtains all of the ordinances of the temple with the promise of all the blessings of eternal life" ("Why Every Member a Missionary?" *Ensign,* November 1997, 35). We must nourish our converts by giving them real opportunities to serve in the Church. By doing so, we are offering them the chance to learn the gospel, deepen their testimonies, and find joy serving in the Lord's kingdom.

9

CONVERTS NEED FRIENDS

After joining the Church I had a transitional experience with a former pastor, one whom I had assisted for several years as an altar boy. I had received my patriarchal blessing eighty-nine days following my baptism and was thrilled at its inspired counsel. I had not known the patriarch beforehand, but that did not matter. He knew the Lord, and the Lord knew me. This humble patriarch made many pronouncements that were able to comfort and guide me throughout my life. I think it was a divine rendezvous that he gave me the blessing three days before I received a long letter from Father Graff.

Father Graff, as any church leader might do, was trying to recover me from what he perceived as a tragic, even spiritually fatal, error of leaving my former church. "Did your parents fail to teach you the lesson that your first obligation was to save your immortal soul in and through the Catholic Church?" he asked. "Your trust should be in your God, the God of your faith which you received at the time of your baptism into the Catholic Church." He quoted Matthew 6:25–27, 31–33 in an effort to convince me to seek first the kingdom of God. "To renounce your inherited faith in favor of someone else's is not true. No man can be happy if he throws away the only sure means of obtaining happiness in this life and in the next, his faith. In the name of the Holy Family, Jesus, Mary, and Joseph, I beg you to reconsider your course of action. It is not too late now, it will be later." It was signed, "Your former pastor and friend."

I knew he was sincere and was reaching out to me in a way he thought was best. But I had found the truth and could not back down from my convictions despite my respect for and relationship with Father Graff. I had learned and would continue to learn that converts encounter opposition to their desire to find the truth. It is as the prophet Jacob in the Book of Mormon said when challenged by a nonbeliever: "He had hope to shake me from the faith" (Jacob 7:5). This is a universally common occurrence for new converts. The support system of nourishment, friends, and responsibility must be well in place early in the process of coming into the Church. Luckily for me, when Father Graff's letter arrived, I was not shaken enough to return to my previous religious life. I was founded in the truths beyond the traditions and religions of men. I was staying with the First Vision, the restoration of the priesthood of God, the additional testament of Jesus Christ, and other latter-day scriptures. I was sticking with the restoration of the true church and the plain and precious doctrines of Christ. I wanted to be a Latter-day Saint, live my new-found religion, and follow the living prophets and apostles. It was a time of testing and a time of moving on in my new faith.

CONVERTS NEED THE SUPPORT OF GOOD

FRIENDS TO ESTABLISH ROOTS IN THE GOSPEL.

Converts through the ages have all faced the challenges that come from living their newfound truth. That is why the prophet, President Gordon B. Hinckley, has counseled that every convert must have a friend. However, much of what is involved with being a good friend to our prospective members and new converts involves our willingness to rely on the Lord and use faith in our efforts. Joseph Smith said, "Doubt and faith do not exist in the same person at the same time; so those persons whose minds are under doubts and fears cannot have unshaken confidence; and where unshaken confidence is not there faith is weak; and where faith is weak the persons will not be able to contend against all the opposition, tribulation, and afflictions which they will have to encounter" (*Lectures on Faith* [Salt Lake City: Deseret Book, 1985], 6:12). We must really believe that this is the work of Jesus Christ, that He has asked us to help Him move the gospel cause forward with faith, and that we are empowered to assist others in coming unto Christ. When our testimonies are strong, then we can offer to share the burdens of our prospective members and new converts by loving and friendshipping them. Jesus said, "My yoke is easy, and my burden is light" (Matthew 11:30). We must be willing to bear each other's burdens. In so doing we will receive the help we need from Christ. The Lord opens doors for us. To the apostle Peter the Lord said three times, "Lovest thou me?" And three times the Lord responded to Peter's answer with "Feed my sheep" (John 21:15–17). The Lord has said that He knows His sheep. He invites those who will hear His voice to join His church. He has asked us to shoulder part of the responsibility to recover His lost sheep and to keep them in the fold.

In the Book of Mormon we read that the faithful missionary Ammon faced trying times with the people he taught, but his faith in the Lord was strong. He said, "When our hearts were depressed, and we were about to turn back, behold, the Lord comforted us, and said: Go amongst thy brethren, the Lamanites, and bear with patience thine afflictions, and I will give unto you success. And now behold, we have come, and been forth amongst them; and we have been patient in our sufferings, and we have suffered every privation; yea, we have traveled from house to house, relying upon the mercies of the world—not upon the mercies of the world alone but upon the mercies of God. And we have entered into their houses and taught them, and we have taught them in their streets; yea, and we have taught them upon their hills; and we have also entered into their temples and their synagogues and taught them" (Alma 26:27–29).

Once the commitment has been made and a person is baptized, we must not give up our efforts. Nurturing through friendship and sharing is vital to the new convert's success. New converts are fresh and eager to live according to the truths they have just learned about. Exercise the faith required to know how to be a friend, how to take care of our converts after baptism, and how to help nurture their newly formed testimonies. A new convert's growth can come from the strengthening qualities of good friends in the gospel.

Now, let us take a journey across the United States as we peek into the landmarks and roots of the Restoration. After we familiarize ourselves with where the Restoration took place, let us then examine the role of friendship in reestablishing the Savior's true religion on the earth.

I-90 traverses America from east to west, from the Pacific Coast to the Atlantic Coast. Literally thousands of exits are provided. Major cities are located along this historic interstate highway, such as Boston, Albany, Syracuse, Buffalo, Cleveland, Chicago, Madison, Sioux Falls, Rapid City, Sheridan, Missoula, Coeur d'Alene, Spokane, and Seattle. Millions of people, all children of our Heavenly Father, travel I-90 day and night, day after day, year in and year out. They are going somewhere, coming from somewhere, being tossed to and fro with every wind of doctrine like the bushes and trees blown and whipped by the thousands of vehicles that rush by on this great highway.

Westbound on I-90, after Syracuse and before Rochester, a single exit sign carries the name "Palmyra." This is a tiny town, lying beside the old Erie Canal, dotted with monuments called churches and rich with history of the doctrines of men, having a form of godliness but denying the power thereof.

In about 1815, Joseph Smith's family came to this quiet place. God prepared a marvelous work and a wonder in this obscure wayside. There is a forest glade there, reverently called by Latter-day Saints the Sacred Grove. The God of heaven and His holy Son, Jesus Christ, beings beyond description, full of light brighter than the noonday sun, appeared to the boy-prophet right in that place—just off I-90 and just north of that busy highway of life. Think of it! The world again had access to truth about the Supreme Being of the Universe, God the Eternal Father: Our Father in Heaven was again revealed to the fallen and apostate world. Could such a thing really happen in our day? Could God be so profound, so real, so willing to help His children? It did happen, and Jesus was there as well. Jesus instructed Joseph in plainly spoken words, and the heavens were opened again for us. Truth was revealed to a prophet, and even a record was available to testify of the Savior—yes, even another testament of the living Son of God, the Redeemer of the world. Where was the record? In a nearby hill called Cumorah, just off I-90 westbound, right along the Palmyra Road. A record was there, a record seen five thousand years ago by Enoch. It was truth sent forth out of the earth, "to bear testimony of [the] Only Begotten; his resurrection from the dead; yea, and also the resurrection of all men" (Moses 7:62). This sacred record, translated by the gift and power of God and known today as the Book of Mormon, was prepared for mankind near little Palmyra. It was published to the world right in this little town.

Let us leave I-90 for a moment and pick up I-80 south of Syracuse and just into Pennsylvania. Here we find Harmony. It is not even identified as an exit, but this is the place of the restoration of the holy priesthood, called today the Aaronic and

Melchizedek Priesthood. There is a river there, the Susquehanna, on whose banks holy events took place in which God's authority was restored to man and sacred ordinances were performed as Jesus would direct. So much good for so many people—for all the people of the world—yet it is hardly noticed by the masses who hurry to their busy lives, their self-declared forms of worship, and their worldly distractions.

Returning to I-90, before we leave New York state, the sacred record called the Doctrine and Covenants, section 20, leads us to another scene so small it is also not mentioned on the highway exit signs. In fact, it is not mentioned in many road maps of New York state. I refer to Fayette, New York. This tiny place, the simple log home of Peter Whitmer, was the location of many sacred events. The testimony of the Three Witnesses was signed there, the Book of Mormon translation was completed there, the Church was organized there, twenty revelations in the Doctrine and Covenants were received in that home ten miles south of I-90, just east of Palmyra. It was a remarkable time of schooling for the Prophet Joseph Smith. He was now twenty-four years old, and the heavenly process had begun when he was fourteen years old with the remarkable vision of the Father and the Son who appeared to him in the Sacred Grove. On Tuesday, April 6, 1830, with nearly sixty people crowded into the humble cabin, the church of Jesus Christ was again established upon the earth by proper authority and with the ordinances necessary for salvation. The restoration of the gospel was well underway.

Real places, real people, real authority, real revelation to do God's work in the latter days. If we hurry on westward and cross Pennsylvania into Ohio, we will find another sacred place. Watch for the exit off I-90, where hardly a public notice appears. There it is—*Kirtland*—Kirtland, Ohio. Sixty-six revelations were received in the vicinity of this hamlet. More doctrines of the Restoration were revealed there. Angelic beings with keys of authority and the truths of eternity were brought from heaven to the Prophet Joseph Smith in this place. Jesus came here, and Joseph declared, "He lives! for we saw him, even on the right hand of God; and we heard the voice bearing record that he is the Only Begotten of the Father" (D&C 76:22–23).

The first latter-day House of the Lord was erected in this little place. Moses, even the mighty prophet of Israel, came to this temple—Elias and Elijah also. They revealed wondrous blessings from the eternal throne of God. That's right—it happened at Kirtland, just off I-90, east of Cleveland, a little to the south of that main thoroughfare traversing America east to west. The magnificent libraries of the world do not hold these secrets of the kingdom of God. Not even the mighty cities of the world were the places of the restoration of the eternal gospel. The mysteries of the kingdom of God were revealed in Palmyra, Fayette, Harmony, Kirtland, Nauvoo, and even today in Salt Lake City.

Though I have seen the places of the Restoration, have stood on those sacred spots, and have trodden the Holy Land of America and the ancient Holy Land, or today's Israel, I knew before I visited where Jesus walked and prophets talked that the events of the Restoration and the Lord's life were *true*. I bear witness that I knew it was true before I saw the places with my eyes, before I felt the feelings in those places in my heart. The Restoration did occur—just off I-90, in holy places, in our day. I know by the power of the Holy Ghost that these things occurred, that Jesus is the Son of God, that this is His church, that Joseph was His prophet, and that the Book of Mormon is another testament of Jesus Christ, proclaiming the Redeemer's holy life and teachings. This is His church and kingdom on earth today. I write reverently of Jesus and Joseph. For me, their names are inseparably linked as friends of all mankind. Jesus taught Joseph, and Joseph taught the wondrous revelations of the Restoration.

These events did not occur without some difficulty and

persecution, however. The road was long and hard as Joseph Smith and the other believers worked to establish the Lord's church on the earth. Joseph Smith was the first latter-day example of a truly retained convert. As Jesus is the prototype of salvation or a saved Being, so is Joseph the prototype of converts in the restored gospel of Jesus Christ. His father and mother and other members of the family were also valiant in their conversion to the Lord and the restoration of all things in these last days. New converts often feel somewhat the way those first members of the Church might have felt—unsure of the doctrine, infantile in experience, and even alone in their efforts. The story of Joseph Smith's brother Hyrum provides some insight into how Joseph was able to withstand the pressures of a newfound religion.

Joseph had a challenging life as he decided to stand by his vision once he had committed to the process of restoring the gospel of Jesus Christ. Among the first to challenge his revelatory experiences were the ministers of the local churches. Most converts are tested as to whether they will have the strength to stay committed. One poignant relationship through all of this difficulty for Joseph was with his brother Hyrum. Through the years of establishing the Church, Hyrum stood by Joseph, sustained him, and supported him. They were faithful in the gospel together. Fourteen years after Hyrum stood with Joseph as one of the first members of the newly organized church, they faced the greatest trial of their lives: death at the hands of those who opposed this restored religion. When Joseph knew he was going to be killed, he begged his brother to return to safety, but Hyrum would not leave him. The scripture records, "In life they were not divided, and in death they were not separated" (D&C 135:3). From the time of his conversion, Joseph had a friend who was willing to stand by him and never leave his side. That friend helped him in all aspects of his life—even until their tragic death in the Carthage Jail.

I also feel honored to call Joseph *my* friend. I have come to know the meaning of the words penned by John Taylor after the Prophet's death. He said, "Joseph Smith, the Prophet and Seer of the Lord, has done more, save Jesus only, for the salvation of men in this world, than any other man that ever lived in it" (D&C 135:3). I cannot express adequately my love for this friend of all of us who have found the joy of the restoration of the true gospel of Jesus Christ.

What about our convert friends? Will we help them, love them, and nourish them—never giving up on them? Will we help sustain them through their trials, hardships, and difficulties as well as their joys? I regard my brother Jerry as one of the most valiant of latter-day converts and a true friend to me. Since his conversion, we have been able to share a brotherhood of the highest respect and regard. One year after his baptism, he served as a faithful missionary in the Franco Belgium Mission. This was made possible by members of an elders quorum who contributed the funds for his service. Just days after he returned from the mission field, he was called to serve his country in the Vietnam War. He did so as a medic and as an ordained seventy. He taught the gospel in foxholes, bomb craters, and jungle camps and was regarded by his companions as a faithful and devout follower of the Lord. Miracles were part of this man's daily walk in the hazards of war. He has married in the temple and raised a beautiful family of missionaries and examples in gospel living. We have both served as bishops, in stake presidencies, and on high councils, and we have performed temple work for our deceased ancestors. How I love faithful and obedient Gerald S. (Jerry) Coleman. To be with him, or hear his voice, or anticipate time together with him is one of my greatest joys in this life. I feel sweet nourishment from his faith and humble testimony and friendship. Jerry stood with me in my decision to join the Church. He still stands with me, and I with him. We are brothers in flesh and brothers in the gospel. Oh, what a difference dear friends and family make in a convert's ability to stay committed to the decision of baptism!

Another good friend in the Church is my wife. The Lord led me to the gospel through Judy England, and together we grew in knowledge and understanding through courtship, temple marriage, and raising a family. We have served and studied and prayed our way through the challenges and joys of this life. I was very fortunate that this friend, who introduced me to the restored gospel, has become my eternal friend and companion.

John Madsen and I have also followed similar gospel paths. One of my first gospel education experiences was attending his seminary class. If you remember, that is where I gained a testimony of Joseph Smith. Isn't it interesting that I have followed him in his vocational pursuit. I am grateful that he encouraged me to enter the Church Educational System as he did when we were young married men. We both served as Church leaders and full-time mission presidents. Our families were together often in pursuit of masters' and doctorate degrees in education. I consider it a great honor that we have grown and served together in the work of the Lord. Perhaps the greatest blessing we could share in this life as eternal friends came when we were both called to the Second Quorum of the Seventy in June 1992 and to the First Quorum of Seventy in April 1997. Two men, one baptized by the other forty years ago, now serve full-time in the latter-day work of our Master and Savior.

I pay tribute to these three special friends, my faithful brother, my eternal companion, and my steadfast mentor. They have supported my search for the true ways of the Lord. What greater friends could a convert have? They helped me establish deep gospel roots, and I have been strengthened by their love and companionship during these years of enjoying the blessings of the restored gospel of Jesus Christ. May we be the kind of friend to new converts that will strengthen them and support them in their newfound religion as my friends did with me.

10

THE WORD OF GOD IS SWEET NOURISHMENT

After my baptism in November 1962, I was like a human sponge. I could not absorb enough of the truths of the restored gospel of Jesus Christ. The new doctrine, the clarity of the gospel, along with teachers and leaders who shared this influence with me were filling my cup to overflowing. I noticed that my new friends and leaders were often going to Lewiston or Moscow for "leadership training." I wanted to go also, but I was not a leader. So, I asked if I could just ride along and learn from my peers by association. They took me with them to Lewiston. I would sit out in the car as the meetings began. On an occasion or two, someone would come outside and invite me to sit in the back of the chapel during the general training. Then they would dismiss to other more specific meetings. Again, someone would see me alone at the back of the chapel, in this unusual circumstance, and invite me to be part of one of the meetings going on in another room. It was glorious! I was learning and growing and finding my way into the Church. I was being nourished by the good word of God. It was like a constant spiritual rush to become acquainted with the scriptures, an expanding view of life, prophets, and eternity. So much clarity, purpose, and plainness flowed into me, things of power and light and truth that have changed my life for the good.

About eighteen months after my baptism, I began working for the Church Educational System. Six years into my employment, I was invited to attend a stake conference outside of my own stake where an apostle of the Lord would be presiding. The stake president drove up to the building with the Church leader, and as they got out of the car, Elder Spencer W. Kimball stepped up to me and said, "I did not know you would be here. I would like you to be my companion this weekend, and I want you to stay right by my side in all of my meetings and responsibilities." I could hardly comprehend what he was saying. President Johnson never did figure it out either because I was a definite tagalong for the next two days. But I did as Elder Kimball requested and was in every meeting with him.

As the conference sessions concluded on Sunday afternoon, he and I were walking through the chapel on the way to the car that was waiting to take him to the airport. He suddenly turned to face me, took me into his arms for a big hug, and thanked me for being his companion. I felt that I had just experienced one of the great moments in time with a living prophet of God. I knew that I had been taught at the feet of one of the Lord's leaders. I was growing. I was strengthening my testimony and understanding of the gospel. I was being nourished.

Other experiences in the Church led to further nourishment. After my baptism, I made a habit of traveling to the general conferences of the Church as often as possible. While attending a conference, I would gain great insight into the lives and manners of the leaders of the Church. Many of them would stroll through the aisles and greet the Saints and friends for many moments before the proceedings began. It was gratifying to see the love and respect they had for each other before and after the prayers and talks were given. There were handshakes, pats on the back, whispered words of encouragement, hugs, sharing of the big red chairs before a prayer was given, and all kinds of appreciation and camaraderie shown. It was a joy to be in the Tabernacle and experience firsthand the spirit of the conference of the Church. A thrill always went through me when the First Presidency came to the stand and the congregation would rise in reverent respect for them. There were many messages spoken and unspoken that were associated with the worldwide general conference, which was attended by the members from across the earth.

On one occasion, while living in Spokane, Washington, I made the trip to Salt Lake City on Friday for the conference weekend. As Saturday morning came, I was up early to drive to Temple Square, but not nearly early enough. The crowds were already filling the square, and long lines were forming in front of all the doors to the Tabernacle. In fact, the line outside door number 10 was clear across Temple Square and halfway down the south side of the Assembly Hall. I was shocked. It was only 8:00 A.M., and I was in a line full of people and nearly three hundred feet from my goal. During the next thirty minutes we moved up in the line thirty or forty places. The usher called out that the Tabernacle was full and that we should all go to the Salt Palace for a seat. I wanted to be in the Tabernacle, but it didn't look promising. Another fifteen or twenty minutes went by, dozens of people dropped out of line, and I inched forward. Again the usher declared that the building was full and that there was no reason to stand in line. More people fled to other places for a seat, and I moved up again. It was now 9:00, and several dozen people were in front of me. It looked hopeless. One by one those in front of me straggled away until by 9:30 only a handful remained at door number 10.

The clock ticked on, and by five minutes before the hour, I was the only person standing in front of the chosen door. Again the door opened, and the usher looked out and into my eyes. He said, "Are you still here?" He closed the door, and my heart sank.

In a few more moments the choir began to sing the opening hymn, right at 10:00 sharp. Surely there was room for just one more person to sustain President Harold B. Lee, the new prophet of God. As the hymn neared conclusion, the door opened one more time, and the usher beckoned me inside. He placed me on half a seat and behind a post, but a welcome seat it was. How grateful I was to raise my arm to the square that special day in sustaining the Lord's chosen leaders in that historic place. My faith was increased as my efforts to gain entry were rewarded. The nourishment by the good word of God continued.

CONVERTS NEED OPPORTUNITIES TO LEARN
THE GOOD WORD OF GOD IN ORDER TO
CONTINUE GROWING IN THE GOSPEL.

Such is the growth that can come from giving our new converts opportunities to be trained, taught, and nourished by the good word of God. Many of the opportunities for my learning revolved around being educated in the responsibilities of the priesthood to which I had been ordained. The restored gospel brought with it the authority to act in the name of Christ. This is important, because without it, it would not be possible for ordinary mortals to accomplish the work of the Lord that is required of us. The great power that makes all of this happen is the power that pushes the Lord's work forward in this life and on the other side of the veil between mortals and immortals. It is also the power that performs the ordinances of eternal life, that preaches the word of God, and teaches the doctrine of Christ. Jesus said to the Nephite disciples, "I give unto you power that ye shall baptize" (3 Nephi 11:21). Further, he declared, "Blessed are ye if ye shall give heed unto the words of these twelve whom I have chosen from among you to minister unto you, and to be your servants; and unto them I have given power that they may baptize" (3 Nephi 12:1). The priesthood in this church is the power of Christ. "And it came to pass that thus they did go forth among all the people of Nephi, and did preach the gospel of Christ unto all people upon the face of the land; and they were converted unto the Lord, and were united unto the church of Christ, . . . according to the word of Jesus" (3 Nephi 28:23).

The power and authority of God was restored to Joseph the Prophet in these last days. In the same manner that Jesus gave this power to disciples of old, He also gave the priesthood to His servants in these latter days. By the authority of the priesthood, the gospel of Jesus Christ is taught to as many nations as will open their doors to these authorized, ordained, true messengers of the Lord. The true preaching of the word of salvation in Christ can be done only through this church.

The power and authority to perform the ordinances of salvation in the true church and kingdom of God will be found only in the true church. The Church is established through holy ordinances of baptism, confirmation, ordination, and sacraments in memory of the body and blood of Christ, and it is the only true church on the earth today. Further ordinances of eternal life and sealing of fathers and mothers and children to one another for time and eternity are bound by the sacred priesthood power given to man through Jesus Christ in this church. Sacred ordinances in the temples of the Lord, which now dot the earth, are ample evidence of this eternal power and authority. The word of God is taught and administered through the priesthood power.

These truths have been given to me as part of the conversion process. I have benefited from profound learning experiences over forty years of holding, exercising, and honoring the priesthood of God. Did I understand these things as a twenty-one-year-old who was ordained a deacon, then a teacher, then a priest, then an elder? No. But as conversion is a process, so is coming to understand and use the power and authority of God a process, a growing process. I had to be taught these things in order to truly understand them. I had good friends who let me walk by their side and learn from them. I put myself in places where I would be taught the good word of God. Such is our role in the life of converts after baptism. We must not give up on them. We must teach, guide, support, and sustain them.

My gospel education did not stop at baptism. In reality, it had just begun. This is often the case for converts following their decision to be baptized. Teach them. They will need education in the doctrine as well as the social and cultural realities of the Church. The language we use in the Church is often confusing to new members. Jargon such as Mutual, Primary, Young Men, Young Women, stake dance, General Authority, Sharing Time, fast and testimony meeting, and so forth are just the beginning of a wide range of cultural references used in the Church. We can help nourish new converts in these social adjustments as well as teach them the doctrine of the restored gospel. The prophet Moroni saw our day and how to strengthen the members of the Church. He said, "After they had been received unto baptism, and were wrought upon and cleansed by the power of the Holy Ghost, they were numbered among the people of the church of Christ; and their names were taken, that they might be remembered and nourished by the good word of God, to keep them in the right way, to keep them continually watchful unto prayer, relying alone upon the merits of Christ, who was the author and the finisher of their faith" (Moroni 6:4).

Our friend Nancy, whom we talked about in chapter 2, likened her conversion to living a fantasy. She was courted and loved into the Church. After baptism, she felt forgotten and abandoned, lonely and uneducated. She wondered about her place in the Church, but her testimony was founded on the principles of the gospel of Jesus Christ. This foundation aided her growth in the gospel despite the fact that she felt alone.

She was also blessed to have a friend named Sue who helped nurture her in the word of God. Sue was the early morning seminary teacher for the ward at the time. If that wasn't service enough, she offered to teach any Relief Society members the seminary lesson each morning after the regular seminary class was over. Nancy attended this class each day and grew in the gospel as she was nurtured by the good word of God.

Our convert friends need us just as much as our investigator friends. Nourish them, love them, and teach them the good word of God. Never give up on them so that they will never give up on their own budding commitment to the gospel. This nurturing and teaching truly does influence converts long past their dates of baptism.

11

ETERNAL TRUTHS
ABOUT THE FAMILY

Some time ago my family and I were traveling across the state of Washington to visit relatives. At about the midpoint of our journey, I turned off the main highway and proceeded up a winding, narrow, dusty road to the old farm of my youth. The road was familiar, with its rocks and ruts and billows of dust that rolled up behind the car and spread out across the fields. The fields were familiar also, rolling for miles with endless patterns of green and brown woven together in a patchwork of beauty.

The children had never been to the old farm from that way before. It was fun for me to recall the memories and good times of climbing the great haystack rocks that protruded out of the field fifty to eighty feet high and still showed the boy-made monuments at their summit that we built years before. These huge rocks carried the white scars of lightning strikes and the aging of many years.

As we drove down the canyon, we could see the old farm house at the valley floor. The closer we drove to it, the more forlorn it appeared. As we pulled into the weedy driveway, we were filled with emotion mixed with grief at the sight of broken windows, shattered walls, and destruction so thorough as to eliminate any element of beauty that once prevailed there. Even the carved wooden moldings on the doors, windows, and storage areas were ripped out. The old sunporches were torn away, and the ornate posts that lined their shady edges were shattered and broken. There was not a wall, not a window, not a board that did not bear the mark of reckless vandalism.

At that time we had five children, and they all wanted to see the inside of the old home. I carried them in one by one, fearing the broken glass and protruding nails. The most joyous aspect of the entire structure was the robin's nest full of squeaking, chirping, peeping babies. At least the old structure yet provided shelter for them.

As I looked about, I recalled it was here where I had learned sacrifice and sharing with a large family. Here I had learned the principle of work. Here I had learned both to give and to receive of the labors of others. As a boy I had learned to pray with my family here. The old stove about which we gathered so many hundreds of times was gone also. It seemed that everything once so dear and beautiful was lost forever.

The home had been built in 1913 by my grandfather, grandmother, and great-uncle. My great-grandfather had homesteaded there in the early 1900s. The family had left the Spangle area in Spokane County and lived in a dugout in the side of the hill just south of the big farmhouse. After they decided to work the land and begin their farm life in earnest, they built a log cabin near the spring that feeds the valley. My father was born in the log cabin in 1912. The new frame home was a monument to the hard work and pride of these early settlers of Douglas County.

Questions plagued my mind. Was that all there was to family beginnings? Must our families and our memories fade away and deteriorate as the old farm had done? I thought of these questions and the answers to them that are found in the great and glorious plan of our Heavenly Father.

The Lord's plan includes a much greater purpose than what

we found in the old farmhouse that day. Eternal life with God is His answer to family life. Three of the children raised on that humble farm to hardworking parents are members of The Church of Jesus Christ of Latter-day Saints. Of those three converts, one was a daughter, Mary Kathleen. After graduating from St. Joseph's School of Nursing in Tacoma, Washington, she married Glenn Wiese, a friend of ours over many years. The couple moved to Graham, Washington, where they began raising a family of four boys and two girls.

As years went by, my brother and I sought opportunities to introduce her family to our new way of life. Finally the day came when the Lord opened a door to her heart through a question I posed to her about the concept of the eternal family. I asked, "Will you be with your family forever?" She wasn't sure she would, though she truly hoped she could be. When the missionaries called upon her family a few days later, her four-year-old son, Scotty, welcomed them with open arms, thinking they were his uncles. Having entered the home, these elders began to teach her family. She and her husband and children responded to the missionaries and accepted the restored gospel. Their progress was manifested as they accepted callings in the Church. Their circle of friends and influence widened. Nurturing and growth was alive in their lives and the lives of their six young children. A year after their conversion, they were able to attend the Idaho Falls Temple. They were so talented and offered so many gifts in the service of others and the Lord.

Several years later, in the fall of 1980, while Glenn was serving as bishop in the Graham First Ward in the Puyallup Washington Stake, a serious auto accident in central Washington took the lives of both him and Kay, leaving the six children alone. It was a time of deep mourning for the loss of these choice parents. Searching for answers and solutions to everyday needs and caring was thrust upon all those concerned. It was not easy to carry on, but the gospel had been established in the home of Glenn and Kay Wiese. They had been to a temple of God and had entered into sacred and eternal covenants as husband and wife. They had gathered their children about them in the Lord's house, and by the priesthood authority of God the children had been sealed to their parents, and an eternal family was established. Tragedy could not change the binding power of holy ordinances accepted and lived in this life and assured in the life to come.

THE CONCEPT OF ETERNAL FAMILIES THROUGH
ETERNAL ORDINANCES IS THE GREAT HOPE OF
CONVERTS, AND IT CAN PROVIDE STRENGTH AND
COURAGE TO THOSE WHO COME UNTO CHRIST.

Just as the family ties that had been established in the temple were not dissolved, so the destruction of our pioneer home was not the end of our family ties either. In fact, the ties are even stronger now. They are not built upon the handiwork of man but upon the enduring handiwork of God and His eternal gospel. We have learned that the family weathers the tests and trials of time, the storms of the ages, and the destructions of thoughtless men. We have come to know that the family is the nerve center and headquarters for preparing for eternal life. The family endures beyond the ravages of disuse and deterioration. Though buildings and playgrounds and old haylofts come and go with time, through the Lord's plan, enduring family ties go on forever.

So, people continue to search, and questions continue to be asked about the purpose of our lives. "Is this all there is?" they ask. "Isn't there something more?" Day by day we go through the same routine. There are moments to ponder, pauses caused by a break in our schedules, the departing of a loved one, the birth of another, a discouragement, a joy. Questions can come to our minds and tender feelings to our hearts. Are there answers? There are—beautiful, far-reaching answers. We have the knowledge that can answer these perplexing questions in the lives of our friends and neighbors. Such was an occasion in Halifax, Nova Scotia. One of the unwritten stories that occurred behind the scenes of our temple open house pertained to a newspaper writer. He wrote the following editorial. The headline read:

"New Mormon Temple Tests My Journalistic Powers of Description." He then went on to say, "I'm out of my depth in a big way here. What the heck do I, an occasional Anglican, know about The Church of Jesus Christ of Latter-day Saints? And the answer is, not much. But I'm learning fast, thanks to a rare opportunity for the media to tour the Church's new temple in Cole Harbour. Gathering my courage, I interrupt Elder Gary J. Coleman, the man who's conducting our tour. 'Why do some folks consider you a cult?' I asked nervously about the people known to many non-members as Mormons. 'Why do you people stir such animosity among other churches?' Coleman smiles patiently. 'Because, Peter, we have temples and priesthoods,' he replies. 'Others look at us and say, "They are different." We have gone farther in our use of the scriptures and the prophets.'

"Emboldened, I look around the room in which we're gathered. 'You say you're Christians,' I remark, 'but where are the crucifixes? I don't see any.' Again, the elder smiles. 'Peter,' he says, 'we have many depictions of Christ in the temple. Our focus is on the resurrected, living Christ today, so we don't use the cross. Our center is not on his death.' Wiser but chastened, I shut up so that our tour of this extraordinary place can continue.

"In truth, my first sight of the temple when I swept past the strip malls onto Cumberland Drive was a bit jolting. There it stood, all grey granite and somber. With its soaring column capped by a golden angel, I had a fleeting impression of a war memorial but the inside is another story entirely, as I'm about to see. 'The temple is a place of learning, of instruction,' says the elder, leading us through the glass doors. 'It's a school for the things of God.'

"My first impression is that I've entered a bright but modern funeral home. I struggled to clear my mind and focus on this new experience. Interestingly, the entire temple is divided into rooms. There's no one, pew-filled area of worship like I'm used to. Coleman tells us that entry to the temple is an honour, not a right. It all depends on something called a 'recommend.' 'A recommend says we are worthy to enter the temple,' says the elder. 'It's done by an interview with an ecclesiastical leader. He decides if we are worthy, righteous, and faithful.'

"Our tour continues. The light is bright but recessed, and the predominant colour is a tranquil cream. The thick carpets are a pleasing off-white. Matching chairs and couches are expensive and comfortable. Coleman tours us through rooms with names like 'the endowment room' (where instruction is given into God's plan) and a bride's room. And everywhere we go, we're met by paintings of Jesus: Jesus preaching; Jesus contemplating; Jesus with crowds; Jesus with individuals. More Jesus than I've ever seen under one roof.

"We reach the baptismal area. It's truly stunning, with its small green pool for full-immersion baptisms, but what draws my eye is what supports the pool. It sits on the backs of twelve huge ivory oxen, representing the tribes of Israel. From there, the elder leads us into the sealing room, 'one of the most sacred rooms of all.' This is where covenants are made to bind families for all time. It's here, too, that Latter-day Saints are married. 'The hallmark of our church is the protection and preservation of the family,' Coleman explains, 'not only on this earth but for eternity.' When Latter-day Saints marry, there is not 'till death do us part,' he adds. 'We speak of "for time and eternity," a very different concept than that found anywhere else.' I gazed around. Like many of the other rooms, this one has large, gilt-edged mirrors on the walls. 'Why so many mirrors?' I ask. The elder beckons me to come stand alongside him, midway between two mirrors. He points to our images and how we're reflected into infinity. 'We go on forever,' he says softly. 'Eternity. Unending.'

"Our last stop takes us to the Celestial Room. It's the most stunning of all, dominated by a huge, shimmering crystal chandelier that wouldn't be out of place in the palace of Versailles. Quietly, we take our places on soft couches and large white chairs. There is no talking in this room, only quiet contemplation. This room is trying to impart what it would be like to be in the presence of God.

"There is total silence. Almost. The only sound is me, scribbling away in my notebook. Trying to put words to this amazing place before the power of description escapes me entirely" (Peter Duffy, *Halifax Chronicle Herald*, Halifax Nova Scotia, November 1999).

As the reporter finalized his notes and preparations to leave the temple site, he approached me with a concern. He explained his need to travel to Great Britain to see relatives the next morning. He had already written a piece for the paper to be printed the following Sunday. His concern was that he had strong feelings he wanted to share with his readers while touring the temple. "What should I do?" he asked. I gently counseled that he would not be able to capture those feelings when he returned from his travels. He would need to write about them that night and substitute the article about the temple in place of the article already prepared. Three days later, the temple article appeared in the Sunday edition of the paper. I thanked him for being true to the feelings of his heart.

When we share the gospel with others, we begin to open the doors to eternity. This is one of the most beautiful and hopeful doors we can open. Yet we also begin to help them close doors to traditions of the past. Because of the challenging nature of this task, we must be patient with the process of conversion. It is not an event. The way to help others is to show through our faith and their faith what God requires of them. "Lead me, guide me, walk beside me, help me find the way," says a cherished children's hymn. "Teach me all that I must do to live with him someday" is the plea for our little ones and converts who are asked to become as little children in finding their way back to God and the Lord Jesus Christ ("I Am a Child of God," *Hymns of The Church of Jesus Christ of Latter-day Saints* [Salt Lake City: The Church of Jesus Christ of Latter-day Saints, 1985], no. 301). One convert might come from one family, two from another, and even the whole family might be baptized in yet another instance. The sharing goes on, and each circumstance is different, private, even sacred.

Can you see why the Lord says there is joy in one who comes unto Christ and receives baptism in the true church? These things are true, and the Lord knows that we have the opportunity to be with our families and our loved ones forever, through all eternity. He knows what we must do to obtain this great blessing. We must come unto Him. We must commit ourselves to the gospel truth. We must be baptized and do all we can to bring this blessing into the lives of our friends and neighbors.

I feel so greatly blessed to have come to know the Prophet Joseph Smith as a man God raised up to restore the true gospel of Jesus Christ. I still find it a phenomena of untold wonder that my Heavenly Father would lead me to the doctrines and ordinances of the Savior. He has granted me the eternal blessing of coming out of the world of my circumstances and traditions and into a world of light and knowledge, testimony and peace.

The prophet Moroni, in the closing chapters of the Book of Mormon, made a promise to me and all others who seek for the kingdom of heaven: "And when ye shall receive these things, I would exhort you that ye would ask God, the Eternal Father, in the name of Christ, if these things are not true; and if ye shall ask with a sincere heart, with real intent, having faith in Christ, he will manifest the truth of it unto you, by the power of the Holy Ghost. And by the power of the Holy Ghost ye may know the truth of all things" (Moroni 10:4–5).

Bringing converts unto Christ is a spiritual undertaking. It is also one of the trials of our faith. There are certain divine, eternal truths that God wants His children to hear. I believe that we all heard them before in the premortal gospel training we received. The truths we have known for eons of time may now be suppressed in mortality. They can be recognized, however, when the Holy Ghost stirs the depths of the soul and we hearken to the sweetness of the truths recorded on our eternal spirits. I feel this is what happens when we are brought to a circumstance of hearing the truths of the restored gospel. It is as though we have heard these things before and they are familiar to us. It is as though we have a longing to know the meaning and purpose of life. This longing can be satisfied only through learning the eternal truths encompassed in the gospel of Jesus Christ. President Joseph F. Smith taught, "All these salient truths which come home so forcibly to the head and heart seem but the awakening of the memories of the Spirit" (*Gospel Doctrine*, 5th ed. [Salt Lake City: Deseret Book, 1939], 13).

Anciently, Mormon wrote, "The Spirit of Christ is given to every man, that he may know good from evil; wherefore, I show unto you the way to judge; for every thing which inviteth to do good, and to persuade to believe in Christ, is sent forth by the power and gift of Christ; wherefore ye may know with a perfect knowledge it is of God" (Moroni 7:16).

The gospel of Jesus Christ is true. We enjoy the blessing of belonging to the only true church upon the face of the whole earth. Jesus Christ is our Savior, and it is His work that we share with others. Always the prophets have invited, even commanded us, to seek the Lord. "And now, I would commend you to seek this Jesus of whom the prophets and apostles have written, that the grace of God the Father, and also the Lord Jesus Christ, and the Holy Ghost, which beareth record of them, may be and abide in you forever" (Ether 12:41). We are led by living prophets who expound the restored gospel and teach us the way to eternal life through the Savior. I know the Book of Mormon is true, for I have received the witness promised in the writings of Moroni. Joseph Smith was indeed a prophet of God.

May we sincerely pray that the Lord will help us share these truths with family and friends. May we bear testimony to those whom we fellowship that we have a precious gift that will change their lives and bring them great joy. May we take courage to bring converts to Christ. President Gordon B. Hinckley has extended a powerful invitation to all of us as we face the times ahead: "My brethren and sisters, do you realize what we have? Do you recognize our place in the great drama of human history? This is the focal point of all that has gone before. This is the season of restitution. These are the days of restoration. This is the time when men from over the earth come to the mountain of the Lord's house to seek and learn of His ways and to walk in His paths. This is the summation of all of the centuries of time since the birth of Christ to this present and wonderful day" ("At the Summit of the Ages," *Ensign,* November 1999, 72). Now is the time to share the gospel message and spread the good news of the Restoration. Now is the time to help our friends and neighbors grow in the gospel both before and after baptism, so that they too can experience the eternal joys that the truth can bring.

INDEX

ABOUT THE AUTHOR

Elder Gary J. Coleman was sustained to the First Quorum of the Seventy of The Church of Jesus Christ of Latter-day Saints on April 5, 1997, after serving in the Second Quorum of the Seventy since June 1992. He has served in several Area Presidencies and is currently Area President of the Mexico North Area.

An educator by profession, Elder Coleman has taught in the Church Educational System for twenty-eight years. When called to full-time Church service, he was associate director of the Institute of Religion at Weber State University. He holds a bachelor's degree in physical education from Washington State University, a master's degree in counseling and guidance, and a doctorate in educational psychology, both from Brigham Young University.

A convert to the Church, Elder Coleman was baptized in 1962. Since that time he has been in five full-time mission presidencies, served as president of the California Arcadia Mission during 1987–1990, and was president of the New York Rochester Mission in the spring of 1998. He has also served the Church as a bishop, stake president's counselor, and high councilor.

Elder Coleman was born in Wenatchee, Washington, on September 18, 1941, to Benton Joseph and Evalin Barrett Coleman. He is married to Judith England Coleman, and they are the parents of two girls and four boys. They also have thirteen grandchildren.